SAVING BIG CREEK

How a Persistent Group of Activists Blocked a
Multi-Million Dollar Resort, Rescued an
Endangered Butterfly, and Expanded
Opportunities for Citizen Involvement in Land
Use Decisions in Oregon

SAVING BIG CREEK

HOW A PERSISTENT GROUP OF ACTIVISTS BLOCKED A
MULTI-MILLION DOLLAR RESORT, RESCUED AN
ENDANGERED BUTTERFLY, AND EXPANDED
OPPORTUNITIES FOR CITIZEN INVOLVEMENT IN LAND
USE DECISIONS IN OREGON

ANDREA SCHARF

DANCING MOON PRESS
NEWPORT, OREGON

Saving Big Creek
How a Persistent Group of Activists Blocked a Multi-Million Dollar Resort,
Rescued an Endangered Butterfly, and Expanded Opportunities for Citizen
Involvement in Land Use Decisions in Oregon
copyright © Andrea Scharf, 2018
All rights reserved

Paperback ISBN: 978-1-945587-27-6
Ebook ISBN: 978-1-945587-28-3
Library of Congress Control Number: 2018911092

Scharf, Andrea
Saving Big Creek: How a Persistent Group of Activists Blocked a Multi-Million Dollar Resort, Rescued an Endangered Butterfly, and Expanded Opportunities for Citizen Involvement in Land Use Decisions in Oregon
1. Big Creek, Lane County, Oregon; 2. Counterculture communities; 3. Land Use Decisions and Laws-Oregon; 4. Oregon Silverspot Butterfly; 5. Endangered Species Act; 6. Geologic History of Lane County Oregon; 7. Citizen Activism in Oregon; 8. The Nature Conservancy; 9. Oregon Department of Parks & Recreation. **I. TITLE**

Front cover photo, aerial view of Big Creek: *Peter Vince*
Front cover photo of Oregon Silverspot Butterfly: *Mike Peterson*
Back cover photo: *courtesy of Marie Cole*
Photo of Tom Smith: *courtesy of Billie Jo Smith*
Book editing, design & project production: *Carla Perry*
Cover design/production; interior maps & bridge icon illustration: *Sarah Gayle*
Manufactured in the United States of America

DANCING MOON PRESS
P.O. Box 832, Newport, OR 97365; 541-574-7708
www.dancingmoonpress.com; info@dancingmoonpress.com

FIRST EDITION

FOR TOM SMITH
1930–1991

....to them will be shown the unbroken web of life
and the meaning of infinity.

—Alice Walker
The Gospel According to Shug
from her book, *The Temple of My Familiar*

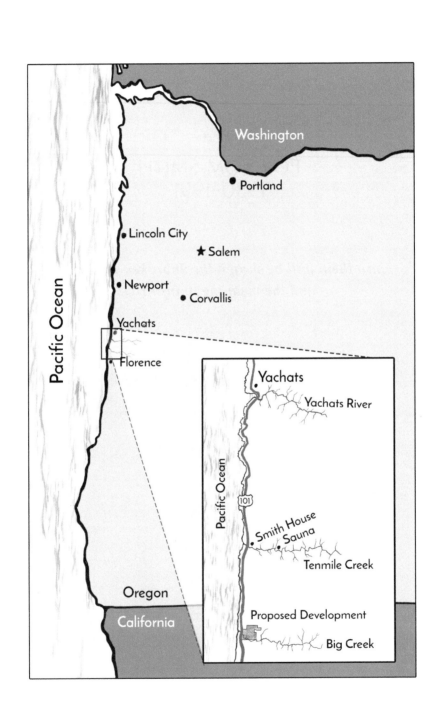

ACKNOWLEDGMENTS

There would be no *Saving Big Creek* if not for the decades of persistent efforts of a dedicated group of activists and the community that supported them, as well as the generosity of individuals and agencies that made it possible for The Nature Conservancy to buy the property and transfer it to the Oregon Department of Parks & Recreation to preserve its natural condition in perpetuity. Too many to name individually, their contributions are, hopefully, honored by this book.

Many people gave generously of their time to answer my questions about the Big Creek acquisition. Others satisfied my curiosity about subjects as diverse as the origin of the Yachats basalts, the sex life of butterflies, the plans for building a nuclear power plant on the Big Creek property, and the tedious work of monitoring land use actions at the county level. Everyone who was kind enough to talk with me is listed in the Interview section. I'm grateful to all of you!

Matt Spangler and Kent Howe, former planning directors for Lincoln and Lane counties respectively, helped me with the history of Oregon's land use laws in general and how they impacted real-life land use decisions. Special thanks to Matt for his careful reading of the manuscript for accuracy. Various agencies helped too—kind people willing to delve into reams of records stored in boxes or digitally recorded.

Special thanks go to three people who supported this effort in so many ways. First, Robert Ackerman loved this project and encouraged me to pursue it. Second, Jim Adler, storyteller extraordinaire, has been artfully telling stories about Big Creek and the Tenmile community for decades and some of those stories are preserved in this book. And finally, thanks go to Billie Jo Smith for sharing the story of her life with Tom Smith with such vivid detail that I sometimes thought I'd actually met him.

Any errors are my responsibility.

Tom Smith

CONTENTS

FOREWORD

Writing about recent history presents interesting challenges. Many of the people involved in the Big Creek project—on both sides of the controversy—are still alive. They were generous in giving me hours of their time to recall and reconstruct their roles in the Big Creek controversy. But efforts to block the development of the resort and preserve the area as natural habitat went on for almost forty years. It wasn't the all-consuming passion of everyone's life—how could it be? People had families, work, and other causes to fight for. Details about who said what to whom, what a hearings room looked like, the weather, even the precise order of events, were overwhelmed by the quotidian facts of life.

But those details are what make an account of the past come alive. I wanted to create a sense of those times at Tenmile and Big Creek, and I wanted to experience it myself, so I imagined how things looked and what people said based on the interviews, documents, and on-site observations. Several people involved in saving Big Creek have read and commented on the manuscript. If something didn't sound quite right, I worked with them to make it more accurate.

~

The balance between using resources so that humans can have the life they think they want, including the leisure to experience the natural world, and yet limiting the use of those resources to preserve the natural world, is not easy to maintain. At one time, it was proposed that a funicular be built to give people access from the floor of Yosemite to the top of Half Dome. An editorial in opposition was written by a man in a wheelchair who believed that preserving wildness, even if people faced a strenuous hike to observe it, was more important than his desire to look down on the valley floor from a great height. People who supported the development of a resort at Big Creek described the developer as a visionary whose lodge would provide accommodations for people right there on that wild piece of the Oregon Coast. Others struggled for years to block construction of a resort and preserve wildness without human intrusion.

Efforts to achieve that balance continue in other locations with varying diverse development proposals. Sometimes the conflict is difficult and prolonged. Even with laws in place to preserve and protect the natural world, it feels as if eternal vigilance is required, and people weary of the struggle. I hope the Big Creek story will inspire people to continue their quest to keep the natural places free, and to provide sanctuaries for all living beings where humans are just visitors who leave no trace.

INTRODUCTION

In 1979, a developer from Honolulu bought 186 acres on both sides of a small creek on the Central Oregon Coast. He planned to build a lodge, rustic cabins, a trading post, and two houses for the future owner/managers. This, he claimed, was his dream—to operate the resort with his wife and another couple when he retired.

The site for the proposed Big Creek Resort was one of the last privately owned, undeveloped areas between Florence to the south, and the village of Yachats to the north. Bordering the Big Creek property are National Forest lands, state parks and campgrounds, a wilderness area, and miles of empty, wind-swept beaches. The country is rugged, with hulking headlands, sharp ridges dark with Douglas-fir, spruce and hemlock, and small creeks and streams that flow into the ocean. Plants—common, rare, or invasive—fill meadows and wetlands, and a small butterfly with toasty brown wings inhabits the salt spray meadows between the forest and the ocean. At the same time that the developer took out an option to buy the Big Creek acreage, the butterfly was being considered for listing as a threatened species under the Endangered Species Act. Any development, or other use of the property, would have to take into account threats to its habitat.

Opposition to the resort grew quickly, but it was dismissed by the developer as coming from "a bunch of hippies."

He was not entirely wrong, although his dismissive tone turned out to be far off the mark. Opposition to the development at Big Creek included many young people who had moved to this part of the Oregon coast in search of a new way of relating to nature and to each other. They built cabins, grew much of their own food, and explored an alternative lifestyle. The developer failed to see the community's strengths. Even though they were dispersed along the several roads that followed the creeks and rivers on this part of the coast, the young people formed a close-knit cohesive group. They lived on Tenmile Creek Road[1] and Big Creek Road, along the Yachats River, and in the nearby community of Yachats. The center of the community was Tenmile Creek Road, a few miles north of Big Creek, where Tom and Billie Jo Smith had settled in the summer of 1976.

Tom, a decade or so older than most of the people in the community, was a treasure trove of experience and expertise. Many of the activists involved in the Big Creek controversy went on to pursue careers on behalf of the environment, crediting Tom with teaching them the skills they needed to be effective. Mostly in their twenties and thirties when the battle for Big Creek began, they had white hair and gray beards by the time the property was finally secured by The Nature Conservancy and donated to Oregon State Parks. Their tenacity is a lesson and an inspiration. Not even Oregon's innovative land use planning law was enough to save Big Creek without the persistent personal commitment of this dedicated group.

~

Property, as Eric Freyfogle reminds us in his book, *On Private Property*, is a social construct. It isn't a fundamental right and it didn't grow out of some misty past. Property exists as a tool by which society determines how resources will be used. In the United States, when homesteaders were needed to occupy the vast "unoccupied" lands to the west, people were encouraged to file claims and settle there. When industrial development became desirable, the supposedly sacred rights of property owners were often abridged in order to facilitate the operations of factories and mines, even if they polluted the water of property owners downstream, or filled the air with toxic fumes and ear-shattering noise. As awareness has shifted to the connectedness of the natural landscape and the potential for unregulated growth to send plants and animals into extinction, not to mention the damage caused to humans from air and water pollution and unregulated disposal of waste, property laws changed again, restricting some uses of the land to achieve social goals.[2]

When Oregon's Senate Bill 100 was passed, it imposed a duty on all cities and counties in the state to develop a land use plan and the appropriate zoning to enforce it. Serious efforts were made to engage the public in determining what those uses should be and where they should be located. This was a revolutionary concept for most of the rural counties of the state, where there was essentially no zoning.

Local plans were still in flux when Victor and Linda Renaghan bought the Big Creek property in the northwest corner of Lane County. Stretching from the peaks of the Cascade Range to the breaking waves of the Pacific Ocean, Lane County was far advanced in some aspects of land use planning, but it was one of the last counties to have its comprehensive plan approved by the state's Department of Land Conservation and Development. Because of its mix of rural and urban land uses, it was also the only county in Oregon that had to meet all nineteen of the state's land use goals. During this period of thrashing out compromises and establishing procedures, there were both opportunities and obstacles for those who wanted to develop their property, and for those who objected to such development.

The property along Big Creek was zoned for timber production and wildlife, not for resort or residential development. The developer therefore needed to obtain approval for a zone change—a quasi-judicial process before an appointed Planning Commission. The hearing before the West Lane Planning Commission would be the first opportunity for the opponents of the resort to make their case. Eventually, the process took them all the way to the Oregon Supreme Court.

Over the next thirty-five years, the two sides strategized and made their moves, each one countered by the other side. Lawyers, planners, bankers, and environmentalists used whatever tools they had to influence decisions about how the Big Creek property would be used. There were successes, and there was frustration and despair on both sides. In the end, the questions of who (or what) would use the property and who could (or should) be involved in those decisions were answered.

~

The legal definition of *standing* is the right to appear in a court of law and be heard. The question of who had standing in the Big Creek case had relevance for the operation of Oregon's land use laws. Eventually, that question was settled in a way that broadened the participation of citizens in land use decisions, providing a strong counter to development interests and expanding definitions of social good.

I have a personal sense of *standing* as a "sixth sense" that would enable me to stand anywhere and know, as if I were actually there at the time, what had taken place ten, a thousand, or ten million years ago. As I researched the Big Creek story, I began to think about what the area was like when it emerged from the primordial sea. What changes in deep time took place here to present the geographical features we see now? Who has occupied the land and for what purposes? Who occupies it now, and how should it be used in the future? This time-affected story entwined itself in the battle to keep Big Creek in its natural condition, whatever that means at this moment in time.

Tom Smith, at the center of the fight to save Big Creek, had perfected *standing* in another sense of the word. Empowered by knowledge of and passion for the natural world, Tom delighted members of the Tenmile community as well as visitors to the area with his ability to stand in one place and talk about everything that could be seen, smelled, heard, felt, or tasted without moving from that spot—from the ground under his feet to the top of a tall tree. Many of the people I interviewed for this book recalled listening to Tom—for hours sometimes—while he stood at the base of a spruce or next to swampy wetlands describing what many of us see but don't notice. Tom's enthusiasm for the natural world, his experience dealing with organizations and agencies in sometimes adversarial conditions, and the respect he engendered among the activists who fought to keep the Big Creek land natural and to protect the plants and animals that inhabited the area, formed the solid foundation on which opposition to the resort was built.

~

Tom died a few years before I arrived on the Central Oregon Coast. I had heard stories about him and felt I knew him, but it wasn't until I began writing the story of Big Creek that Tom really came alive and became a friend of mine too.

CHAPTER ONE
A SMALL CREEK ON THE CENTRAL OREGON COAST

On a map, the rivers and creeks of Oregon's Coast Range look like the veins of a giant leaf. They flow east to the Willamette Valley and west to the ocean from a spine of low mountains that run north and south from the Columbia River to the Umpqua. Tiny feathery blue lines merge with slightly bigger lines and then bigger still, until finally there's a creek worthy of the name. Where the drainage is short and the exit plan is directly into the Pacific Ocean, the creek is considered a tributary to the ocean, commonly called an ocean trib.

Big Creek, in the northwest corner of Lane County on the Central Oregon Coast, is an ocean trib.

Big Creek begins as a seep on the headwall of a canyon—a wet spot under a rock, a little muddy patch under the ferns, a place from which a dribble of water begins to move downhill. There's not much wiggle room between the steep sides of the draw. The trickle is tiny. Trees clinging to the slope shade the nascent creek and sometimes fall, choking the canyon with giant pickup sticks. Another little rill joins the first, and another, until the draw widens and several tiny rivulets flow together.

Watershed managers refer to the drainages as "fields," and assign a number to indicate how far up the network of tributaries their drainage goes. The tiniest creeks are Field 1. When they reach a certain flow, measured in cubic feet per second (cfs) they are numbered 4 to 6. Big Creek is a Field 4 stream, similar to many other ocean tribs along this part of the coast, flowing from the ridges down to the ocean: Cape Creek, China Creek, Big Creek, Rock Creek, Tenmile Creek, Bob Creek, Cummins Creek, Gwyn Creek, another Cape Creek, the Yachats River, Vingie Creek, Starr Creek, another Big Creek, a few more small tribs, and then the Alsea River.

The Alsea is a big river system, covering more than 299,704 acres, with 450 miles of streams in its watershed. The main stem of the river is 43.5 miles long and is navigable to tidewater, about twelve miles from the mouth. The Alsea's broad estuary once supported intensive salmon harvest, canneries, and timber mills. Now it's a popular location for recreational fishing and crabbing, kayaking, and birding.

The misnamed Big Creek in Lane County is a small system. It's one of nine drainages grouped together by the Siuslaw National Forest as part of their Cummins/Tenmile Watershed Analysis. The entire drainage is about 55,000 square miles. Big Creek itself is approximately twelve miles long. It is not navigable.[3]

Most of the small ocean tribs flow right into the Pacific, but Big Creek spreads out near its mouth to form freshwater wetlands before it enters the ocean. The bigger systems, like the Alsea River and the Yachats River, are tidal, flooded diurnally by salt water and forming saltwater marshes. These wetlands are valuable habitat for young salmonids, which use the slow moving water as a refuge during the transition into their ocean-going adulthood. At Big Creek, a rise at the mouth blocks the salt water. Without a salt marsh to provide a sheltered nursery, the fish in Big Creek have had to adapt. Since the fish have been returning to this river to spawn for hundreds of thousands of years, they have created a unique subspecies that foregoes the usual saltwater transition.[4] At one time, great numbers of Coho, Chinook, Steelhead, and cutthroat trout thrived in Big Creek, just as they did in most of the ocean tribs. Big Creek used to be a popular fly-fishing stream, but the fish populations are now greatly diminished.

From the moment I decided to tell the Big Creek story, I began stopping along Big Creek Road whenever I traveled south on U.S. Highway 101. At milepost 175, just north of Conde McCullough's graceful bowstring arch bridge, I turn left, cautiously, because the asphalt has eroded, creating a tire-eating pothole just past the junction. Soon the asphalt gives way to gravel as the road flattens out, then climbs along the north side of the river.

It's a pleasant walk nearly any time of the year. Usually I see no one. Occasionally there's a fisherman walking along the road, or a pickup truck goes past; we wave the way people do on rural roads. My dog busies himself exploring scents and occasional deposits of scat. About half a mile in, old fishing trails lead down to the river and a couple of abandoned campsites. Water seeps out everywhere, merging with the fast-flowing creek. Logs crisscross the creek, slowing the flow, creating quiet backwaters where young fish find refuge during high water, and capturing gravel and cobble where hen salmon dig nests, called redds, in which to lay their eggs.

In the spring, the world is new and very green. Great shiny leaves of skunk cabbage emerge in boggy areas. The waxy yellow bracts shelter a stem of tiny flowers like a lantern protecting a flame from the wind. The smell is sharp, pungent, not unpleasant, although the odor of the flower itself is more appealing to flies, attracted by the smell of rot.

Catkins appear on the willows, male on some plants, female on others, soft and fuzzy, stroke-able as a cat's tail. The triumphant triple-leaved trillium, its creamy-white three-lobed flower nodding on a slender stalk, pokes out of the ground under the firs. Delicate in appearance, the wet leaves are crumpled until they finally spread out to reveal the lovely flower. Under ideal conditions, a trillium can live for eighty years.

Soon there are small flowers scattered like rice at a wedding; the leaves and stems commingle in an orgy of green. Some are as small as my fingernail. I look them up in the *Audubon Guide to Western Forests*, trying to match pictures with the truth on the ground. The names are like the *dramatis personae* in an Elizabethan drama: Queen's Cup, Bishop's Cap, Monkshood. The disloyal courtiers are False Lily-of-the-Valley, False Miterwort, False Solomon's Seal. Tiny drops of deep magenta, delicate white stars, spikes of pale chartreuse. Yellow Violets, Western Bleeding Heart, Redwood Sorrel, Yerba Buena, Miner's Lettuce and Rattlesnake Plantain, Saxifrage and Vanilla Leaf, the latter used by early settlers to freshen their laundry.

I remember the stories my friends have told me about looking for the elusive and bizarre Long-tailed Wild Ginger, used by early settlers to spice up their food. The expeditions were led by Tom Smith, a naturalist and a teacher, and as I mentioned earlier, legendary for his ability to stand in one place and rivet everyone's attention for hours, guiding his audience from the fungus and rhizomes under the ground to the tangled mat of groundcover plants. From the ferns, salal, Oregon grape, all the shrubs and bushes, and right up the rough trunks of fir and spruce to the canopy where, with a little luck, a flying squirrel would leap out and coast from one tree to another.

I could use Tom's expertise now to identify the riot of plant growth, although there's also pleasure in just observing the splash of color, clueless as to name and function. The temperate rain forest explodes with life after the gray winter months. All too soon, the green begins to overwhelm. Everything leafs out, until I can no longer parse the details of the landscape or even see into the near distance. Every opening created by floods, landslides, fire, and logging is filled with a thick understory, penetrated only by animal trails. Salmonberry, blackberry, and thimbleberry thrive anywhere trees have been removed, anywhere sunshine can reach. I can easily imagine the despair of the early settlers who battled without pause against the vegetation that threatened to engulf their homesteads. In what seems to be a mild, innocuous landscape, the profusion of plant life feels as if it is intent on evicting the intruders.

The deciduous trees leaf out—delicate light green vine maple, chartreuse serrated lobes of alder, wide hands of the big river maples, elderberry that will soon sport clusters of berries, red and bitter, not the sweet purplish berries used to make elderberry wine. Cascara is also found in open ground. The bark's medicinal qualities were an important source of cash income for the homesteaders, and an essential item in the Native people's medicine cabinet.

Leaves push the catkins off the willows. Willows, which contain salicylic acid, the active ingredient of aspirin, were also used as medicine by Natives and Euro-Americans. Willow branches were woven into baskets and used to frame fishing weirs.

Some plants in the area are neither useful nor beautiful. Recently, giant knotweed has invaded the lower reaches of Big Creek. It presents a daunting challenge to the Forest Service, State Parks, and The Nature Conservancy, all trying to find a method of eradication that won't harm aquatic life. Besides the plant's ability to reproduce itself with the smallest straying bit of root, giant knotweed grows right at the edge of the water, which means spraying herbicides is out of the question. A member of the *Polygonaceae* family, giant knotweed has been used as an ornamental and has some medicinal uses, but is classified worldwide as a highly invasive species. Its growth is so dense that it crowds out every other plant, even blackberry. Once the knotweed leafs out, the river is obscured behind the dull uniform green of its large leaves, which rustle in the slightest breeze. The whisper of the leaves seems malevolent to me, an alien presence that threatens the health of the ecosystem and won't go away.

In summer, the Oregon Coast is cool. Marine air is drawn onto the land as the Willamette Valley, on the east side of the Coast Range, heats up. Fog blankets the firs and drips from the needles onto the ground, a precious source of moisture during the summer when it doesn't rain much. Waves roll onto the beach from the north, carrying the sand that had been stripped away during the winter back onto the shore. The appearance of the beach changes as the sand buries cobbles and basalt outcroppings, the ancient stumps of trees, and driftwood from ferocious coastal storms. A thin, cold wind, originating in the Gulf of Alaska, blows off the ocean, forming delicate sand sculptures in the lee of every shell and rock on the shore.

With less rain, the river's flow decreases and the mouth of Big Creek changes too. Shifting sand redefines the creek's channel. The winter winds pushed up a berm on the south side, forcing the river to turn north. In summer, the water flows more directly west to the ocean. Sometimes there's not enough flow to push it all the way on the surface. As the tide ebbs, Big Creek quietly sinks into the sand.

When autumn arrives, the deciduous trees fade away into splotchy yellows and browns; no one takes a fall color tour of the Oregon Coast. The leaves are stripped off by the first big storms in November. Branches crash. Huge old trees are blown over, leaving their shallow root wads exposed. Soggy leaves, needles, and branches begin to break down, enriching the soil and providing a nursery for young seedlings. Fall slides into winter as warm, rain-saturated air—the "Pineapple Express"—moves in over the land. The winds shift around to the south. Miles up Big Creek valley, you

can still hear the roar of the surf. By four in the afternoon, it's dark.
Chilly and damp, winter persists for the next five months. Again, I
wonder how the early settlers survived.

~

The view to the east from the middle of the Big Creek bridge
overlooks a freshwater wetland where the river meanders as it
spreads out along its floodplain. On the right is a steep, densely
forested ridge that forms the south side of the Big Creek drainage.
The forest that was clear-cut seventy years ago is now a plantation,
a monoculture consisting almost entirely of Douglas-fir. Newer
management policy encourages planting a mix of species—fir,
spruce, red cedar. In areas disturbed by clear-cutting or landslides,
red alders take hold naturally, unless they are deliberately
discouraged by applying herbicides. Once considered a weed, red
alder has found an economic niche for value-added wood products.
It takes a stain well and can be used for furniture. Occasionally, it's
worth more than the fir. But the real value of red alder is its ability
to fix nitrogen in the soil, adding significantly to the health of the
forest. There is very little alder on the south slope.

Only a few scattered remnants remain of the ancient forest that
once covered the Coast Range. Some of it burned in natural or man-
made fires. Most of it was logged, not once but twice, and in some
cases, the plantations are third generation trees. Under current
policies of the Siuslaw National Forest, clear-cut timber harvest has
given way to selective cutting to allow the forest to recover from the
intensive harvests of the past sixty years. In the clearings, sunlight
penetrates to the forest floor, allowing the understory to recover,
which provides shelter and food for a variety of animals. The
remaining trees will be allowed to mature. The intent is that, at least
on federally owned land, the ecosystem will eventually resemble
the healthy natural forest that once blanketed the Coast Range.

From the moment Euro-American settlers saw the trees of the Coast Range, they recognized the value of this region for timber production. Eighty inches of rain fall on the western slopes of the Coast Range annually, pushing the signature tree, Douglas-fir, *Pseudotsuga menziesii*, to immense heights. Old growth Douglas-firs soar to 200 feet, rivaling even the coast redwoods in awe-inspiring size. The diameter at the base of a mature tree ranges from two to five feet; some giants are much larger.

Where the ridge south of Big Creek nears the ocean, the trees are warped by the wind, pushed and prodded into shape as if someone had applied styling gel. Finally, they give up altogether and the vegetation shifts to dense thickets of salal and the low groundcover plant community of salt-spray meadows. Bisected now by the highway, these salt-spray meadows are a unique ecosystem. Salt-laden rain, elk and cattle, fire, and mechanical mowing have suppressed all but a few hardy plants. Historically, this allowed a small slow-growing plant with blue-violet flowers to propagate and survive. Upon this violet, *Viola adunca*, the larvae of the Oregon Silverspot Butterfly dine when they emerge from their nine-month hibernation. They eat voraciously before moving to the pupa stage. After ten days to two weeks, the brownish-orange butterflies emerge to fight, love, and die. Development, tourism and recreation, and highway traffic have reduced this habitat and brought the butterflies close to extinction.

The land on the north side of Big Creek Road appears strikingly different from the south ridge. A low rise of humpy ground is covered with spruce and hemlock, their gnarly branches twisted by the wind and bearded with pale chartreuse-colored lichen. The topsoil is thin, and roots are shallow. Winter storms hit the slope with full force, causing windthrow—the heavy crashing of branches and entire trees. Unlike some trees in the Coast Range, spruce doesn't need fire for its seeds to germinate. As the downed logs decay, they create what little soil there is above the basalt. Seedlings take root on fallen logs and old stumps, known as nurse logs. An old logging track, overgrown with young alder, leads to a small open meadow. Power lines buzz overhead. The ground is moist, with puddles where water can't percolate beyond the layer of soil.[5]

Along Big Creek Road, the cutbank reveals roots growing sideways, blocked by the basalt layer. Several small creeks emerge from the north-side slope and flow under the road, through culverts, into the wetlands. Elk have churned up the duff and broken trails down the bank to the road on their way to browse in the wetlands. Occasionally, there's a small herd on the road, five or six cow elk trying to decide whether to go back up into the trees or out into the wetlands to graze on grasses and sedges. A female Roosevelt elk weighs between 575 and 625 pounds, yet they seem to melt soundlessly into the forest when I get too close. The bull elk is bigger, weighing up to 1100 pounds, with antlers up to five feet from tip to tip. He may be hidden in the trees further up the hillside, watching over his harem—but he too can slip between trees as quietly as a breath of warm air. When these huge animals break into a run, there's a sudden explosion of noise as branches crack and break.

Just off the highway is a flat area where people park before crossing the highway to scramble down to the beach. Road crews store their equipment there when repairing the road or, as they did in 1996 and 2014, cathodizing the supports for the bridge. One of the early homesteaders, Amel Stonefield, had a house here, but it has disappeared, along with a few other buildings, all overwhelmed by vegetation, vandalism, and the harsh marine weather.

Like most river valleys in the Coast Range, Big Creek is not a pristine area. Humans have used it for ten thousand years, though their impact was slight until about 150 years ago. Our knowledge is limited, but it appears that Native people visited Big Creek mainly for summer food gathering.[6] Beginning around 1840, Euro-Americans hunted and trapped, logged, built homesteads, and grazed cattle. Houses and fenced fields have been part of the landscape since the end of the nineteenth century and, since 1933, a major north-south highway separates the wetlands from the coastal prairie and the ocean shore.

Most of the land surrounding the mouth of Big Creek is in the public domain—part of the Siuslaw National Forest or Oregon State Parks. To the north is the Rock Creek Wilderness Area. Campgrounds and roadside rest areas are hidden behind screens of dense vegetation. There are no houses or stores, no motels. There is often no one on the narrow strip of cobble and sand at the ocean's edge, no one along the creek.

At night, there are no visible lights. The wind, blowing through the trees along the ridge, or rustling the bushes along the creek, is constant. The ocean pushes onto the land, a loud roar, or a soft susurration. Big Creek feels like a wild place.

CHAPTER TWO
COMING SOON—BIG CREEK RESORT

On a storm-battered January day in 1981, Tom Smith was struggling to keep his old VW bus on the road. Wind and rain, roaring across miles of ocean, slammed into the vehicle. Trucks, each one carrying 80,000 pounds of rain-soaked logs south to the mills in Florence or Coos Bay, threw off spumes of water as they passed. There were few other cars.

Tom forced the wheel to the left, then whipped it back to the right to maintain his lane. Waves of water overwhelmed the puny windshield wipers. He felt as if he was driving blind through a car wash. As he crossed the bridge over Big Creek, he barely registered the wooden sign that had sprung up out of nowhere. He didn't think he'd seen it that morning as he drove south. He was late getting home, thinking about what he could put together for dinner for Billie Jo and the kids, and anyone else who might drop by, as people often did around suppertime. With this storm, he thought, probably it would be just the family.

The Smith family had arrived on this part of the Central Oregon Coast, an area known as Tenmile for the creek that emptied into the Pacific at that point, five years before. Billie Jo was a highly qualified teacher who had been the environmental studies coordinator for a federally funded project affiliated with the University of Minnesota. She developed curriculum and supervised teacher training, but she'd only recently found a comparable job in Oregon. She had been so frustrated trying to get an Oregon teaching certificate that she was ready to give it up and become a barmaid.[7] Fortunately, after a stint as a half-time teacher at the small Yachats Elementary School where she taught music and took over the fifth and sixth grade students when their regular teacher shifted to her other role as the school administrator, Billie Jo began working at the Lincoln County School District offices developing curriculum and instructional resources.

She worked in Newport, which was a forty-five minute drive each way. Sometimes she carpooled, sometimes she drove the VW bus, but that bus had been a lemon even before they drove it out to Oregon. The last time it died on her, she left it in Newport and bought a new car, a red Honda Civic. Eventually, they retrieved the bus and that was Tom's transportation when he needed it. Tom drove the local school bus, took care of their daughter Rachel, fed the goats and chickens, planted the garden, and had dinner ready for Billie Jo and the older kids when they came home from school.

After wrestling the VW through the storm, Tom parked it in the barn and dashed into the house. He was standing at the kitchen counter slicing broccoli, carrots, and turnips, soaking the bolete mushrooms they had picked and dried that fall, when sixteen year-old Ian came in, shaking water out of his hair. The house smelled of damp wool, wood smoke, mold, chamomile, and sour milk. Ian hung up his wet Army jacket.

"Hey, Papa," Ian called, walking through the house to find some dry clothes.

"There was a sign up at the mouth of Big Creek," Tom called after him. "Something about a resort. I didn't get a good look." He glanced at the clock above the sink. Just enough time. "Want to come along?" He put brown rice and water into the big cast iron pot, brought it to a boil, then turned it down to low. He and Ian ducked out the back door and climbed into the van.

Tom turned left into the pullout north of the bridge where Amel Stonefield's house had been and angled his headlights at the sign: Coming Soon BIG CREEK RESORT. There was a crude drawing of the bridge, and a phone number with an 808 area code.

Father and son shared a look. "I thought this was Forest Service land," Ian said.

"We'd better find out," Tom said. It was fully dark by then. They drove back to Tenmile to finish preparing supper.

CHAPTER THREE
ON THE EDGE OF THE CONTINENT

Once upon a time, when dinosaurs roamed Montana and pterosaurs ruled the skies, there was no Oregon.

—Ellen Morris Bishop, *In Search of Ancient Oregon*

That's the very big one.

—Kathryn Schulz, referring to the possibility of a major subduction event in the Pacific Northwest in "The Really Big One," *The New Yorker*, July 20, 2015

Big Creek Resort wasn't the first recreational development planned for this area of the Oregon Coast. In 1969, the Eugene Water and Electric Board designed a beachside resort as part of its plans for a nuclear power plant on the remote Big Creek site. But before we look at that history, let's step back several hundred million years to see how this part of the Oregon Coast evolved.

More than one hundred million years ago, the best beach real estate in Oregon was in western Idaho.[8] A shallow tropical sea lapped the shore and extended westward to cover nearly two-thirds of the globe. The Cascades didn't exist, nor did the Coast Range. North America had only recently been ripped apart from the single land mass of Pangaea—recently in geologic time, that is. The violent processes that made the Earth look like something we would recognize today were colossal, but they happened over periods that are as alien and incomprehensible to us as the amplitude of space or the minuteness of atomic particles. If you're not an astrophysicist, or a nuclear physicist, or a geologist, all of it seems too big or too small or too remote in time.

Clues to how the planet came to look as it does now are often buried beneath earth-shattering, deep-time events. Even a geologically recent event, the 1700 Cascadia Subduction earthquake, was unknown until recently because it was not recorded in writing accessible to Euro-Americans. However, the terrifying shaking, the sinking ground, and the devastating waves that swept away entire villages were memorialized in the oral traditions of the Native people. At the same time, in Japan, there were records of a mysterious tsunami that arrived from the other side of the ocean, without an accompanying earthquake. But until about thirty years ago, it was thought that the Pacific Northwest coast was relatively stable. We know better now because we know more.

Geologic ages are named: the Devonian is part of the Paleozoic, which stretches from 542 Mya (millions of years ago) to about 251 Mya. Pangaea, the super continent that included Eurasia, North America, South America, Africa, and Antarctica, was stretching like pizza dough, enlarging the land mass as the plates that made up the planet were pushed apart by ridges beneath the ocean. North and South America were separated by one or more ocean plates; they weren't connected until much later, in the Pliocene, a mere 5.3 to 2.5 Mya.

Under the Atlantic Ocean, sea floor spreading from the Mid-Atlantic Ridge, which forms the eastern boundary of North America, began pushing the land westward. The land is still moving. If you drive east across Idaho, you are traveling in the opposite direction of the North American land mass, which slowly and inexorably is grinding its way west. Similar formations under the Pacific Ocean power the shifting shape of the landmasses on both sides of the Pacific.

While the North American plate was moving west, several smaller plates offshore began moving east, forcing undersea real estate up against the continent. These exotic lands are called terranes. A terrane stands out from its neighborhood because it came from somewhere else, pushed into the existing continental crust by the movement of those plates. Terranes began to accrete to North America during the Mesozoic (251 Mya to 65.5 Mya), adding material in the Western Sierras, the Klamath Mountains, the Blue Mountains, and the North Cascades. During that time, dinosaurs flourished and mammals began to make their appearance.

Caught between a rock and a hard place, the land folded and faulted. Mountains rose and fell and re-located, leaving mysterious clues for geologists to find millions of years later. During the Cretaceous (144 to 66 Mya), the coast was still located east of the present-day shore. It extended in a northeast-southwest alignment, from Ashland through Dayville or Mitchell, all in present-day Oregon, and then slanted northwest to Bellingham, Washington, and British Columbia. The land encircled a large bay similar in size to the present Gulf of Mexico, according to Jim Jackson, adjunct professor of geology at Portland State University, who walked the Big Creek property with me and, drawing on scraps of paper, illustrated how modern Oregon emerged.[9]

Sometime in the Eocene, between 60 and 50 Mya, volcanic eruptions under the ocean sent a massive terrane of marine basalts, known as the Siletzia formation, flowing eastward to accrete to the continent in the forearc of the Cascadia subduction zone. Professor Jackson noted wryly, "The plate tectonic model for Siletzia is a somewhat unsettled matter." To put it bluntly, the origin of these oceanic eruptions is unclear. Eventually, the Cascade volcanics and other younger sediments covered up most of the Siletzia terrane.[10]

Following the eruptions of the Siletzia volcanoes and the Western Cascade volcanoes, the Pacific Coast began moving west. It also began to make a clockwise rotation, pushed and pulled by the San Andreas Fault off the coast of California, and the Juan de Fuca plate to the north, shifting like a slow-moving hinge toward the southwest and forming a broad shallow embayment between the Western Cascades and the Coast Range. The area left behind when the waters drained is the Willamette Valley of Oregon.

The rotation began at about the same time a plume of molten material from the Earth's mantle breached the surface in eastern Oregon near Steens Mountain, about 18 Mya. The mantle is the molten material between the Earth's crust and its core. By 15 Mya, the plume was in the vicinity of the Wallowas and Hells Canyon, where most of the Columbia River Basalt Group was erupted. The land kept moving west, but the relatively stable plume stayed in place. It is now known as the Yellowstone Plume or hotspot, the geologic spigot below Old Faithful and the eerie bubbling pools that exhale their vapors from the depths of the Earth.

Massive quantities of lava from the Columbia River Basalts, flowing about as fast as a human could walk, covered much of the Pacific Northwest. Moving down an ancestral Columbia River, the lava flows reached the sea within weeks of the eruptions. This basalt is exposed along the Oregon Coast as far south as Seal Rock, about ten miles south of Newport. Geologists speak of Yachats Basalts, named for the small village of Yachats ten miles north of Big Creek. These rocks form the headlands on the central coast, such as Cape Perpetua and Heceta Head. Further south, however, in the vicinity of Big Creek, the rocks originated from the Siletzia eruptions.

The whole process was messy, cataclysmic, radical. Ellen Morris Bishop uses words like *chaos, deformed, mashing, slapped carelessly, regurgitated, contorted, colliding* to describe how the area we know as Oregon came to look the way it does today.[11] The process left geologists scrambling for explanations. How could Devonian limestones be found next to rocks that formed in the Permian, when the Devonian and Permian geologic periods were separated by hundreds of millions of years? The science of plate tectonics, which provided the explanation, didn't emerge until the late 1960s. Before that, the notion that continents float on plates that slam into or slide over or under each other, was regarded as a totally crackpot idea.

Although others had noticed the jigsaw puzzle fit of the east coast of South America with the west coast of Africa, the theory of continental drift wasn't formulated until a German meteorologist named Alfred Wegener, recuperating from a wound during World War I, began looking at evidence from other disciplines to support the idea that the two continents were once joined. He observed that the lands near the matching coastlines, now separated by thousands of miles of the Atlantic Ocean, displayed similar geologic forms as well as identical plant and animal fossils. There was no way those species could have been transported such distances. They had to have originated in the same place, and then somehow drifted apart.

In 1915, Wegener published *The Origin of Continents and Oceans (Die Entstehung der Kontinente und Ozeane)*. One might have expected his theory to click into place as neatly as those formerly interlocking coastlines, but it did not. Wegener's contemporaries believed the continents and oceans were firmly attached to the planet, and that the ocean floor was a flat surface of thick sediments. No one, not even Wegener, could come up with a plausible force that would have induced those continents to move.[12]

Slowly, in the kind of time we humans understand, scientific developments began to provide the instruments that would gather the evidence. As scientists began to measure and map the ocean floor, and look at geological data, support grew for the theory of plate tectonics.

Deep-sea echo-sounding surveys gradually established a new picture of the sea floor. It was neither smooth nor flat. It had no thick layer of sediments that had been there since the planet formed. Instead, great mountain ranges were discovered in the Atlantic and Pacific Oceans, about midway between the continents. These mid-ocean ridges are continually being pulled apart along the crest as new magma rises up, erupts, and fills the space between the diverging plates.

Evidence shows that rocks are older the farther away they are from the ridge crest. The youngest rocks exhibit normal present-day magnetic polarity, but stripes of rocks further away alternate between normal and normal-reversed polarity, corresponding to shifts in the Earth's magnetic field that cause grains of magnetite in the volcanic rock to line up to whichever way the Earth's polarity is aligned at the time the magma was ejected from the ridge. The magma cooled and locked in the alignment of the grains. It's like having a time stamp documenting when each eruption occurred.

By the late 1960s, scientists had confirmed Wegener's theory. Core samples were lifted from the deep ocean floor and dated— further evidence that the seafloor is indeed spreading and that new crust is continually being created along the mid-oceanic ridges.

The next question was—where does the newly created crust go? The idea that the planet was expanding like a balloon and that was causing the continents to pull apart fell flat. Harry H. Hess, a Princeton University geologist, and Robert S. Dietz, a scientist with the U.S. Coast and Geodetic Survey, proposed that the spreading crust eventually dropped off into the deep narrow trenches along the rim of the ocean basins and returned to the mantle, which was then cycled back up into new eruptions along the ridge.

Scientists got better at measuring earthquakes during the twentieth century. In the 1960s, the Worldwide Standardized Seismograph Network was established to monitor compliance with the ban on aboveground testing of nuclear weapons. Now seismologists could locate the precise zones where earthquakes occurred. Those zones coincided with the oceanic trenches and ridges.

One of the zones was the west coast of North America, moving westward at the speed at which a fingernail grows, about an inch a year. The Pacific plate was moving obliquely in California, along the San Andreas Fault. The Juan de Fuca plate was slipping east beneath the Pacific Northwest margin of North America. The pressures were immense, causing faulting and folding that is visible in much of the convoluted landscape of the Pacific Northwest.

Not until the late 1980s did evidence begin to emerge that a very big earthquake and tsunami had hit the Pacific Northwest coast in the fairly recent past. Brian Atwater, a geologist with the U.S. Geological Service and an affiliate professor of earth sciences at the University of Washington, found proof that the ground along Neah Bay in Washington State had sunk suddenly and that saltwater had rushed in, killing vegetation.[13] First Nation stories told about a deadly fight between Thunderbird and Whale. In one variation, Thunderbird drops Whale from a great height, causing the land to shake and the waters to recede.[14] Seismologist Ruth Ludwin collected the stories and was able to estimate a date somewhere around the beginning of the 18th century. Atwater and David Yamaguchi, a graduate student, discovered a ghostly forest of dead cedars. Analysis of the growth rings showed that the trees had died suddenly, between the summer of 1699 and the spring of 1700.[15]

The exact date of the Cascadia earthquake was January 26, 1700. We know this because written accounts in Japan at that time reported damage caused by a tsunami. The Pacific Northwest quake generated waves that traveled across the Pacific Ocean, arriving in Japan ten hours later. In Japan, it was called the "orphan tsunami," because there was no local earthquake associated with it. Working backwards, bringing together all the evidence, Atwater and his colleagues in Japan established the precise date and time of the "Big One" of 1700, and in 2005 published their findings in a book, *The Orphan Tsunami*.[16]

Knowledge about plate tectonics, the Cascadia Subduction Zone, and the big earthquake of 1700 put an end to the mistaken belief that the Pacific Northwest was seismically calm. But in the late 1960s, in an age of innocence when nuclear power was seen as the perfect way to support anticipated growth in Oregon and Washington, no one even knew that the Cascadia Subduction Zone existed.

On the east side of the Coast Range, at the south end of the Willamette Valley, the public utility for the city of Eugene, the Eugene Water and Electric Board (EWEB), selected several possible sites for a nuclear power plant to serve the Eugene-Springfield area. Among the options was a remote corner of Lane County where Big Creek tumbled out of the Coast Range and flowed into the Pacific Ocean.

CHAPTER FOUR
THE NUCLEAR POWER PLANT

Supply System bond marketing was a study in opacity.
— Daniel Pope, "A Northwest Distaste for Nuclear Power"

It was an incredible fight to overcome EWEB's plans.
— Jane Novick, community activist

In 1969, Big Creek was seriously under consideration as the site for a nuclear power plant. As with many of the hydroelectric dam projects in the Pacific Northwest, plans included public recreation.[17]

The Eugene Water and Electric Board (EWEB), a municipal utility serving the city of Eugene, Oregon, asked voters to approve a city charter amendment that would allow the utility to borrow $225,000,000 to construct a 1,000 MW nuclear power plant. The proposed site was near Coburg, just north of Eugene. Voter approval was an overwhelming 80 percent, but within a few months, serious opposition developed.

A group of citizens, organized as the Eugene Future Power Committee, began appearing at EWEB board meetings and Eugene city council meetings, demanding answers to questions concerning safety and health. Farmers in the Willamette Valley didn't share

EWEB's enthusiasm for using the cooling water for irrigation. Sportsmen were concerned about the effect of the eighty-degree water on fish—salmon need cold water. Eugene residents feared that emissions from the plant and from the cooling lake would exacerbate the already bad air quality that resulted from temperature inversions, and the fact that everything, including thick clouds of smoke from field burning in the Willamette Valley, ended up in the bowl created by the mountain ranges that surround the city on three sides.

The Eugene Future Power Committee brought together University of Oregon physicists, nuclear biologists, and a young architect who knew a lot about heating systems, to analyze EWEB's growth projections. EWEB claimed that "the lights would go out" after 1976 if the plant wasn't built, a prediction based on findings from the Bonneville Power Authority, which operated more than thirty hydroelectric plants serving Oregon, Washington, and parts of Montana, California, Nevada, Utah, and Wyoming.

The Northwest Hydro-Thermal Plan projected construction of one nuclear power plant every year from 1970 to 1990, with five of them located at the south end of the Willamette Valley. EWEB figures showed that population and consumption would increase by ten percent; the Eugene Future Power Committee analysis showed usage increasing by only three percent. National strategies calling for regional industrialization meant power was needed for operation of aluminum plants to be constructed along the Columbia River. A hefty portion of the money raised by the EWEB bonds would go to Portland General Electric for a thirty percent share of the power to be generated by the Trojan nuclear plant that PGE and Pacific Gas & Electric were building on the Columbia River north of Portland. Eugene ratepayers were going to subsidize power that would serve not just the residential requirements of Eugene, but the greater needs of the entire Pacific Northwest grid. These were privately owned utilities. Could money generated by Eugene ratepayers be spent on a private utility project?

The exaggerated projections of the Northwest Hydro-Thermal Plan led directly to the disaster of the Washington Public Power Supply System's nuclear construction program. The entity, known as WPPSS, and regrettably pronounced "whoops," pulled in most of the public utility districts and private utilities in Washington State, and some in Idaho and Oregon. When cost overruns and management errors led the executive director of WPPSS to recommend a moratorium on plants 4 and 5, ratepayers appeared to be stuck with $23 billion dollars worth of debt and debt service to pay back the bonds issued for the projects. According to Daniel Pope, a University of Oregon professor who has written extensively about the WPPSS disaster, "In some small towns where unemployment due to the recession was already high, this amounted to more than $12,000 per customer."[18] Ratepayers revolted.

A young resident of Springfield, Oregon, named Peter DeFazio, who went on to serve as a Commissioner for Lane County and then Congressman from the 4th district, filed a suit against the Springfield utility. The lawyer representing DeFazio was Robert Ackerman, a Eugene attorney who eventually became a state representative. In 1982, Ackerman questioned another public bond issue—to finance construction of a resort at Big Creek. But that's getting ahead of our story.

The Eugene Future Power Committee pressed for hearings, dialogue, answers to their questions. When EWEB evaded those requests, the EFPC decided to put an initiative on the ballot for the May 26, 1970 primary election. The campaign was intense on both sides. Charles O. Porter, a Eugene attorney who also went on to represent the 4th Congressional District, warned EWEB that it was unlawful to use ratepayer funds for their political campaign against the initiative. Experts were brought in on both sides, including people from the Atomic Energy Commission, which was charged with both regulating and promoting nuclear power. As Jane Novick, one of the organizers of the opposition (whose husband, Aaron, had worked on the Manhattan Project and experienced the same dismay that most of his colleagues felt after the first A-Bomb was detonated) pointed out, there was a serious conflict in the dual roles assigned to the AEC.

Stone & Webster, one of the biggest, most successful engineering services companies in America, was hired by EWEB to evaluate alternate sites for the power plant. The firm, which provided engineering, construction, and environmental expertise, plus plant operation and maintenance services, had played a significant role in the development of the atomic bomb.

As soon as the Coburg site was off the table, the farmers' objections disappeared too. Perhaps, EWEB's management thought, moving the plant as far as possible from population centers, especially Eugene, would answer some of the safety concerns. Perhaps it was just a NIMBY issue—Not In My Backyard. The nuclear plant would be acceptable if it were out of sight. They had agreed to keep the plant in Lane County, which stretches from the crest of the Cascade Range on the east across the fertile Willamette Valley to the Pacific Ocean on the west. Candidates for the prize of being chosen for the first EWEB nuclear power plant included Oakridge, a timber town on one of the passes across the Cascades; Noti, another small timber town in the Coast Range; Cottage Grove, a small town south of Eugene; and a place called Big Creek, twelve miles north of Florence in the far northwest corner of the county. In early 1970, EWEB announced that Big Creek was their preferred site.[19]

EWEB touted the benefits of combining recreation with power generation.[20] Just as the lakes created by damming rivers for hydropower have become big recreation sites in the Northwest, so too would the cooling lake for the nuclear plant. Boating, fishing, swimming, camping along the shore, and the growth of tourist facilities in nearby towns would attract millions of users and boost the economies of rural areas; the same positive impacts would accrue to the coastal communities near Big Creek. No one mentioned the possibility of radiation in the water, although there were concerns raised about low-level emissions from the plant itself. But way out on the coast? What damage would that do? There was virtually no one around to breathe the air, and anyway, "low-level" didn't sound all that bad. What could go wrong?

The astonishing thing is how innocent—or ignorant—people were at the time. In the material that the Future Power Committee published to gain support for their ballot measure, there was barely a mention of meltdowns, mechanical or human failure, certainly nothing about the wisdom of perching a nuclear power plant on the edge of the continent. But then, this was 1970. Three Mile Island was nine years in the future, Chernobyl sixteen years, and the disaster at Fukushima in the distant 21st century. Plate tectonics was still a fairly new theory, and the connection between subduction zones and tsunamis wasn't established until the early 1980s.

EWEB's conceptual drawing of the Big Creek generating plant looks like a bizarre forecast of the Big Creek Resort that would be proposed ten years later. The plans included a 2,000-acre lake with swimming beaches, a golf course, duck hunting area, high-rise hotel, beachfront home-sites, marina, restaurant, and a seaplane dock. The plant itself sits like a malevolent black box at the east end of the lake[21], which is, of course, the cooling lake for the plant. The Pacific plate, grinding and sliding its way under the North American plate, is not in the picture.

After an intense period of getting enough signatures to put Measure 52 on the May ballot, followed by the Committee's equally intense campaign to educate the voters of Eugene about the measure, it squeaked by with just 858 votes, 11,750 to 10,892. The measure imposed a four-year moratorium on construction of a nuclear generating facility in Lane County.

Meanwhile, construction of the Trojan plant on the Columbia River north of Portland proceeded with huge cost overruns. The 1980 explosion of Mount St. Helens cracked reactor rods and caused a nine-month shutdown while repairs were made and structural changes installed to accommodate the movement of a fault line that ran underneath the plant. That same year, Oregon voters passed an initiative to permanently ban construction of nuclear power facilities in the state. At about the same time, the WPPSS meltdown began, creating the biggest default on municipal bonds in the country's history. In 1986, Trojan was shut down permanently and the cooling tower, long an iconic symbol of both the nuclear power dream and the nuclear nightmare, was imploded in 2006.

EWEB never took out an option to acquire the Big Creek site. The utility shifted to a conservation strategy that obviated the need for more power plants. John Reynolds, the architect and heating engineer who played a strong role in analyzing EWEB's earlier claims about the need for the nuclear plant, was elected to the EWEB board, the first person who was not a businessman to serve in that position.

CHAPTER FIVE
THE TENMILE COMMUNITY

Back in June 1976, Tom and Billie Jo Smith still hadn't found a house in Oregon. Their VW bus was packed with everything they owned, plus Tom's three children from his previous marriage, and Rachel, two years old, born during the four years he and Billie Jo spent in Minnesota.

They drove through the Willamette Valley and then along the winding roads of the Coast Range, looking for rural property where they could have a big garden and maybe raise a few animals. Tom, born in Texas and raised near Ojai, California, had studied fisheries biology at Oregon State University and dreamed of getting back to Oregon. He wanted to live near the ocean, but fall was approaching and they needed to find jobs and get the kids registered for school. So far, they had seen nothing that would work for them.

They drove north from Florence on Highway 101, around jutting headlands, above narrow beaches where Steller sea lions roared and postured. The coast was rugged, with few habitations of any type.

Occasionally they spotted a fragile cabin teetering on the edge of a cliff where surely the next winter storm would send it crashing into the sea. They crossed one creek after another on graceful bridges, occasionally glimpsing a ramshackle house along the creek banks. Neither of them wanted to live on the west side of the highway where the harsh winds and salt spray would make gardening nearly impossible. On the landward side of the highway were steep ridges with impenetrable dark forests of Douglas-fir, cedar, spruce and hemlock. Nothing enticed them.[22]

Sixteen miles north of Florence, they came around a curve. The road dropped gently to yet another graceful bridge across another creek. There was a bench of land here, a space between the heavily treed ridge and the ocean. There were no houses on the ocean side of the highway. On the east side, an old cabin appeared to be on its last legs. (They later learned it was one of the places where workers lived when the highway was being constructed in the 1930s.)

Next to the cabin, set back from the road, was a charmingly weathered wooden house with a hipped roof, deep eaves, a wide porch, and an unobstructed view of the ocean across wild, empty meadows. Behind the house was a cluster of sheds and outbuildings, including a barn. A gravel road bordered the south side of the property—Tenmile Creek Road.

There was a For Sale sign in front of the house.

~

Rex, Tom's oldest son, was eighteen and had already graduated from high school. The other two children, Stacy and Ian, were enrolled in schools in Waldport—Stacy in her junior year in high school, and Ian starting eighth grade. Tom took care of Rachel and the growing collection of goats and chickens. Driving the school bus, Tom got to know everybody along the route, including Stan Poe, an old-time logger with five children and a huge garden. Stan and his wife immediately offered baskets of produce to Tom and his family, since the Smiths had arrived too late to put in a garden of their own that first year.

The Smith family was part of a new wave of "homesteaders," mostly young people with a back-to-the-land ethic, looking for a more authentic lifestyle. They established communes or communities of like-minded folk outside university towns or in remote valleys like Tenmile Creek and neighboring Big Creek. The seismic shifts of the counterculture, with their epicenters in cities and college towns, brought new energy and new attitudes to rural areas. Into a traditional community of loggers, farmers, and fishermen, the newcomers brought a passion for the environment and radical-seeming ideas about work, family, creativity, and recreation.

By the time plans for the Big Creek Resort came to the attention of Tom Smith and the community that formed around the Smith family, the intensity of the counterculture was waning. The war in Vietnam was over. Some people moved back into more mainstream pursuits, while others shifted from protests to constructing a new lifestyle. Tom and Billie Jo had lived through the sometimes violent and often frightening actions and reactions over war and race when they lived in Washington DC. They and their friends and colleagues had first-hand experience with the protests against the war in Vietnam. Ed Chaney, one of Tom's colleagues at the National Wildlife Federation, sent his secretary on an errand during the anti-war protests. She was rounded up along with thousands of others, disappearing into the football stadium for hours while Chaney frantically tried to find out what had happened to her. (She was eventually released.[23]) In the mostly African-American neighborhood where the Smiths lived, local residents surrounded the Safeway market to make sure their only source of decent food wasn't burned to the ground.[24]

What inspired the extended Tenmile community was a commitment to a simpler way of life, with less focus on material acquisition and more on physical and spiritual health. There was pride in learning how to grow and forage for their own food, build and repair their own homes, live off the grid, be resourceful and self-sustaining. There was joy in the new rituals they invented to celebrate birthdays, weddings, births. The women planned their own festivals, gathering in a circle in the big meadow in front of Sarah Scholfield's cabin to celebrate the full moon or the winter and summer solstice.

As the Oregon timber wars heated up in the 1990s, several Tenmile residents got involved in efforts to save old-growth forests from logging. Caroline Bauman, Paul Engelmeyer, and Chuck Willer formed the Ten Mile Association, which won an award from Portland Audubon for their efforts.[25] Training in nonviolence techniques attracted nearly fifty people to the meadow below Sarah's cabin in August 1995.[26] Throughout the Siuslaw and other National Forests, people blocked equipment from logging sites. Some demonstrations were peaceful, but there were instances of violence on both sides.

Efforts to protect the environment coincided with a broader shift in American politics, including new land use laws and judicial expansion of citizens' rights to have a say in how the land was used.

~

Tom was a genial, gregarious, open-hearted man who was forever making new friends, like the two German girls who were hitchhiking through Oregon and stayed with the family for a couple of weeks, maintaining contact for years after. Or the Greyhound bus driver who, if his schedule permitted, parked his bus at the wide spot across from the house and joined Tom for a cup of coffee and maybe a thick slice of homemade bread spread with Billie Jo's blackberry jam. If Tom saw hitchhikers waiting for a ride, he made a plate of sandwiches and brewed coffee for them. When it got dark, if they were still there and it looked like they'd be stranded for the night, he often went back and invited them over for supper and a place to sleep.[27]

When they first moved to Tenmile, Tom thought he and Billie Jo would have a commune centered around their house, but that didn't work out. What happened instead is that the Smiths' house became a central part of a community that included other people along Tenmile Creek Road as well as people from Big Creek, Yachats, and the Yachats River valley. When Tom's daughter, Stacy, and her husband, Chris Graamans, were ready to build their house, a crew of people from the community worked together, like an old-fashioned barn-raising. When Tom and Billie Jo needed a new roof on the old Stonefield house, it became a community project. Always, Tom was the center, "the fulcrum" of the community.[28]

The U.S. Postal Service didn't deliver the mail to people who lived along Tenmile Creek Road. Instead, they picked up their mail from the row of tilted, battered mailboxes at the pullout on Highway 101; it was only natural to drop in and share a cup of coffee with Tom.

Because folks who lived beyond milepost two were off the grid and didn't have phones, they often came to the Smiths' house to use theirs. If anyone in the community needed advice on any subject, Tom was the one they turned to. For his daughter's wedding, Tom invited everybody who lived along Tenmile Creek Road to the reception, held in the pasture in front of the house: old-timers, hippies, retirees, part-timers looking forward to becoming retirees, everybody no matter what they thought of each other. It wasn't exactly what Stacy had in mind, but it was vintage Tom—making sure everybody met everybody else, de-fusing suspicion and ill will. He believed people needed to help each other out. If an ambulance or fire truck turned up the road, Tom jumped in the VW bus and followed them, to see who needed help. When a fire destroyed Herk Martens' house, Tom and Billie Jo took in the whole family until they could find a new place to live. Tom organized contributions of clothing, bedding, furniture—anything they'd need to pull their lives back together.

When the timber wars heated up and Paul Engelmeyer and Chuck Willer began trying to stop timber sales on the Siuslaw National Forest, they didn't know exactly what to do. They turned to Tom.

"Have you talked to the district ranger?" Tom asked them.

They looked at each other. "We can do that?"

"Sure," Tom said. He picked up the kitchen phone and dialed the Waldport Ranger Station, asked for the ranger by name, talked for a minute, then turned back to the living room. "You've got an appointment tomorrow at ten." It was important, Tom explained, to go through the channels, and to build a paper trail showing that you had tried every possible avenue to work with the agencies. It would pay off in the end.[29]

From his work with Trout Unlimited and the National Wildlife Federation, Tom knew the value of a steady approach to social and political change. His influence on the younger members of the community would be vital to the success of the campaign to keep the natural environment at Big Creek from being turned into an urbanized enclave of resort cabins and second homes.

~

One late spring afternoon in 1977, Tom dropped off the Poe kids, who lived in one of the last houses on Tenmile Creek Road. Then he maneuvered the yellow school bus until he could get it turned around and headed back toward home along the narrow, twisting gravel road. When he reached the three-mile post, he saw a young man working in a garden. Naturally, he stopped to introduce himself.

The young man was Steve Cole. His family had bought 320 acres from James and Doris MacCrae, descendants of one of the original Tenmile Creek homestead families. By the mid-1970s, Doris MacCrae had had it with primitive rural life and was ready to live somewhere with electricity. Steve, and his then-wife Marie, moved into the MacCrae house. Marie's sister, Sarah Scholfield, and Sarah's husband lived across from Steve and Marie in the original one-hundred-year-old homesteader cabin. Later, they subdivided the larger property into parcels that were sold or rented to other young people looking to live a more rural life. Those people included Paul Engelmeyer and Mary Scully, and Chuck Willer and Allison Clement. But when they first moved up to Tenmile, Marie remembers, "it was lonely."[30]

Then Steve met the bus driver. Tom climbed out of the bus, a chunky man wearing a flat-brimmed leather hat pulled down over his long brownish-gray hair.

"Hi," the man said. "I'm Tom Smith. C'mon down for supper."

~

Not long after Tom met Steve and Marie, he helped Steve build a sauna on the hill above their house. The Smith house at the west end of Tenmile Creek and the sauna three miles to the east anchored the community and connected it to like-minded people who had moved to the other little valleys along the central coast. Sunday was sauna day. People drove or walked up the road to Steve and Marie's house. Someone would have already fired up the big barrel stove, taking wood from the huge piles around the sauna. Keeping the woodpile stocked was a group effort—there were wood-gathering parties. People brought construction scraps and cedar shakes from old roofs to feed the stove. They organized rummage sales to raise money to buy wood.

Leon Sterner, who moved to Tenmile with his partner, Caroline Bauman, recalled that the amount of money they made was so inadequate compared to the effort it took to put on the fundraising events that they agreed they'd be better off cutting and splitting the wood themselves.[31]

Late in the afternoon, when the stove was red-hot and the walls hummed with the dry toasty aroma of hot cedar, people climbed up the hill behind the house, hung their clothes on pegs under the eaves, and entered the sauna.

Sarah Scholfield traveled to Guatemala when she wasn't living in the old cabin on Tenmile Creek, and she brought back yards of woven Guatemalan fabric. Billie Jo made a long caftan for Tom from a length of black material with white threads woven through it. The neck and seams were brightly embroidered and he always wore this robe to the sauna. He hung it on a peg next to Jim Adler's gray and white striped robe that looked like a Moroccan djellaba, and the two of them clambered up to the top where it was hottest. Adler, a blacksmith, lived up the Yachats River Road with his Swiss wife, Ursula, and made hand-forged fireplace tools for a high-end catalogue company in Portland. He and Tom were always the first in and the last to leave the sauna.

In the middle of the sauna was a cement pool four feet deep, fed by a spring that trickled out of the ground higher up the hill. People got so hot after awhile that they'd jump into the pool to cool off. The water was shockingly, achingly, cold—"an out of body experience for your balls," as one sauna regular put it.[32] People got very good at the art of plunging into the pool and leaping out in one smooth move, accompanied by appropriate screams of agony. The less masochistic cooled off outside on the deck, where their bodies steamed in the mist-filled air. Late one afternoon, they watched as a 400 pound bear loped up the hillside across the meadow from the sauna, so big it simply plowed through the wall of blackberries and salal before it vanished into the trees.[33]

There were stories about the wild orgies of the Tenmile hippies, but in fact, the sauna was a family affair, as were all the other community events. Kids ran in and out, occasionally falling into the pool. Half a dozen adults would leap off the benches to pull them out. "It wasn't a place for adventures," according to Ursula Adler.[34] They were aware of new people who showed up looking for something inappropriate. A subtle tick of the head was enough to alert the men of the community to ask the stranger to leave.

After the sauna, everyone got dressed and hiked back down the hill to the Coles' house for a potluck dinner. People brought fresh produce from their gardens, preserves and homemade sausage, a fresh-caught salmon, or wild-gathered mushrooms. They brought guitars, recorders, drums. In summer, the light in the house faded gradually as the long twilight glowed in the western sky. In the winter, since there was no electricity this far up Tenmile Creek Road, the light came from oil lamps and candles, flickering while rain pounded against the windows.

One Sunday in late January 1981, not long after Tom and Ian had investigated the Big Creek Resort sign, Tony Cole (no relation to Steve Cole) and his family came up to the sauna. Tony and his brother Pip, former members of the Yellow Submarine, an urban commune in Eugene, had bought property six miles up Big Creek Road. They discovered an abandoned house, once the home of Amel and Marie Stonefield, off Highway 101 just north of Big Creek Road. With the permission of Hugh Sherwood, who owned the property at the time, they scavenged the house for materials to build their own cabins.[35]

Tony met Tom one day when he saw Tom's goats grazing in the pasture next to the highway at Tenmile. He had a couple of goats too, and they immediately bonded over shared tips about the care and feeding of goats, how to make yogurt and cheese from goat milk, the usual things goatherds talk about. Tony's girls were close in age to Tom's daughter Rachel, and it was just a natural thing for Tony's family to become part of the Tenmile community, coming for potlucks, solstice celebrations, and of course the weekly sauna.

Tony climbed up to the top row and sat down next to Tom and Jim. Yes, of course he'd seen the sign for the resort. He passed it every day when he picked up the mail or drove down to Florence. He'd called the Lane County Planning Commission and found out the new owners were Victor and Linda Renaghan. They lived in Honolulu and had already applied for a zone change for the property. The hearing was set for February 11 at the West Lane County Planning Commission meeting in Florence.

"We'll want to testify against it," Tom said.

During dinner, they began identifying which agencies to contact, who would make the calls, who would write letters, who would show up at the hearing.

The battle against the resort development had begun.

CHAPTER SIX
LINES OF DEMARCATION

The earth was created by the assistance of the sun, and it should be left as it was... The country was made without lines of demarcation, and it is no man's business to divide it.

—Chief Joseph, Nez Perce

Victor Renaghan worked for the U.S. Customs Service in Honolulu. In 1979, on a trip to the Oregon Coast with his wife Linda, he saw the For Sale sign at Big Creek and took out an option on the property. Their intent was to develop a small, rustic resort they would operate after Vic retired.[36] That would not be any time soon, presumably—he was only forty when they bought the property.

The property that Vic and Linda Renaghan purchased was zoned NR: *Natural resource/timber/prime wildlife combining*. Building a resort was not an allowable use under the NR zone. The Renaghans could harvest the timber, complying with whatever restrictions applied under the state's Forest Practices Act, but they would need a zone change in order to proceed with their plan to develop a resort.

The Renaghans' property at Big Creek was a distinct commodity, its boundaries and ownership history recorded in county deeds. Parcel 1 is described as "Government Lots 3 and 4, Section 15 South, Range 12 West of the Willamette Meridian, in Lane County, Oregon."

The description of Parcel 2 is more convoluted: "The South ½ of the South ½ of the Northeast ¼; the West ½ of the Southeast ¼; the west half of the Southeast ¼ of the Southeast ¼; and the North ½ of the Northeast ¼; all in Section 15, Township 16 South, Range 12 West of the Willamette Meridian, in Lane County, Oregon."

Parcel 3 is "The North ½ of the North ½ of the Northwest ¼ of the Southwest ¼ of Section 12 of Section 14, Township 16 South, Range 12 West, Willamette Meridian, in Lane County, Oregon."[37]

The deed descriptions refer to a method of surveying and recording land that goes back to the Land Ordinance of 1785, passed by the Continental Congress. It was followed two years later by the Northwest Ordinance of 1787, to deal with the vast amount of territory ceded by Great Britain in the Treaty of Paris, which ended the Revolutionary War. The government wanted to settle this area, known as the Northwest Territory, which included the land from Pennsylvania to the Mississippi River. Land was given to soldiers who had served with the Continental Army, and it was also sold to raise money to pay down the government's war debt. A system was needed to describe and record the property transfers.

In the original thirteen colonies, property lines were described by metes and bounds, based on the English system. Metes and bounds delineated property with local landmarks and distances, such as *"Beginning at the old oak tree next to Muddy Creek and continuing 800 feet to the big rock and then 400 feet to the intersection of the Turnpike with Shady Lane...."* Clearly, this wouldn't work in the wilderness beyond the Alleghenies where the land was sold "sight unseen" and there was no one around to record the deeds. (The fact that it was already occupied by various Native peoples didn't appear to be a concern.)

The federal government established the Public Land Survey System and began the daunting task of surveying all the land acquired by the United States, starting with the Northwest Territory and continuing west across the Louisiana Purchase to the Pacific Ocean. The survey began at a point on the Pennsylvania-Ohio border. Lines of longitude (meridians) and latitude (baselines) were identified to serve as the defining north/south and east/west points from which townships were established. In Oregon and Washington, they are called the Willamette Meridian and the Willamette Baseline.

The land was then divided into townships (also called survey townships), with a square six miles on each side. The townships were divided into thirty-six sections, each one a mile on each side and roughly 640 acres. The numbering of the sections follows a Boustrophedon pattern (meaning turning like an ox plowing a field) beginning with one at the northeast corner across the top to the western edge, which was number six, and then reversing direction for the next line—sections seven through twelve; then west, then east, until all thirty-six sections were numbered.

One acre is slightly smaller than a football field. There are 160 acres in a quarter section, which was the common unit for land claims. Forty acres is a quarter-quarter, giving us expressions like "the lower forty," meaning the land lowest in elevation, or "the back forty," meaning the land furthest from the house. "Forty acres and a mule" was the basis of the Union's plan to make formerly enslaved people self-sustaining after the Civil War.[38]

The survey made its way across the country. In Oregon, the Willamette Meridian was established at longitude 45°31'11"N 122°44'34"W. A cedar stake was driven into the ground by John B. Preston, the Surveyor General of the State of Oregon, in 1851, at the intersection of the Willamette Meridian and the Willamette Baseline in the hills west of Portland. In 1885, an obelisk, known as the

Willamette Stone, was erected to replace the stake. Ninety-five years later, this was also replaced, with a stainless steel marker and a bronze plaque that states:

> Beginning here, the Willamette meridian was established running north to Puget Sound and south to the California border, and the baseline was established running east to the Idaho border and west to the Pacific Ocean.

All real property in the states of Washington and Oregon is described in relation to this point.[39]

CHAPTER SEVEN
ENDANGERED SPECIES

Tom Smith turned fifty in 1980. He was seen as a leader in the Tenmile community; most of the others who settled there and along the other creeks and valleys were in their twenties and thirties. He brought credentials and years of experience to the efforts to oppose the resort development as well as other environmental activism.

Before settling at Tenmile, he had worked for a number of environmental organizations and government agencies. At Montana Fish & Wildlife, he had helped develop the Blue Ribbon trout program that designated certain streams as premium producers of game fish, with licensing requirements that brought in additional funds for conservation as well as controls over the number of fishers allowed on such streams. He was the Executive Secretary of Trout Unlimited. At the National Wildlife Federation in Washington DC, he served as the educational director, producing the *Ranger Rick* magazine and developing education and outreach programs for the state affiliates.

After he and Billie Jo moved to Minnesota, Tom developed outreach programs that brought adults and children to the Hennepin County Park Reserve District where they experienced such adventures as snow camping—an activity that resulted at least once in all the campers retreating to the Smiths' living room, located in the Reserve, after tents collapsed under a heavier than expected snowfall. Remembering Tom now, people describe him as a role model whose example helped them be effective in careers in government, for environmental organizations, and as citizen activists. He was the rock-steady heart of the Big Creek campaign, not to mention his central position in the personal and social interactions of the Tenmile community itself.

The people opposed to the development of a resort at Big Creek met with Tom around the Smiths' dinner table to hash out strategies. Tom's experience and energy motivated and guided them through the nearly forty years before Big Creek was finally protected from all future development.

~

The resort wasn't Tom's first involvement with issues affecting Big Creek. In April 1980, the U.S. Fish and Wildlife Service held a public hearing in Newport, Oregon, on a proposal to list a small brown butterfly as a threatened species under the Federal Endangered Species Act. The butterfly's habitat included the open meadows on both sides of Highway 101, from Tenmile Creek south to Big Creek. Tom attended the hearing. Speaking as a biologist, he argued that the Tenmile meadows should be included in the listing, but others felt that the area had already been compromised too much to expect it to recover. Proposals to include it, they said, were just "land grabs" intended to discourage future development on behalf of the people who were already there.[40]

Speyeria zerene hippolyta, commonly known as the Oregon Silverspot Butterfly, is a pretty insect, about two inches or less from wing tip to wing tip. The wings are a toasty brown with black markings. Small white circles—the silver spots that give the butterfly its common name—dot the underside of the wings. Males and females have subtly different markings and the female is larger.

Anne Walker, who monitors Silverspot recovery plans for U. S. Fish and Wildlife, tells groups of school kids that the way to tell boy butterflies from girls is that "the females have big bottoms."[41]

The Oregon Silverspot has adapted to a very specific habitat niche: salt-spray meadows and coastal prairies from northern California to Washington. Swept by salt-saturated rain that blows across the Pacific Ocean from October to May, the meadows appear as patches of open land between the beach and the forest. The natural succession of plant communities, in which the forest would gradually encroach on the meadows, has been curtailed by the harsh climate and by elk browsing the tender shoots of spruce seedlings. In some areas, Native people may have burned to clear the meadows, although there is no good evidence that this occurred along the Central Oregon Coast.

After mating, which often takes place in sheltered forest areas adjacent to the salt-spray meadows, the female Silverspot lays tiny eggs. Anne Walker has photographed Silverspot females in the process of egg laying. When she blows up the photo, the eggs are about the size of the period at the end of this sentence. The caterpillar hatches within a few days, eats the outside of the eggshell, and goes to sleep. It sleeps through the fall, through the violent winter storms, through the spring. When the caterpillar wakes up, it's hungry. It crawls toward a stubby plant, the Common Blue Violet, *Viola adunca*, which also has been dormant during the severe winter weather. Everything is slow, violets and caterpillars developing in sync, the caterpillar waking up, violets leafing out. Each caterpillar needs two to three hundred violet leaves from about fifteen plants before it morphs into the adult stage.[42]

The arrival of European and American settlers disturbed the delicate balance of the violet/butterfly relationship. During the early twentieth century, the Stonefield brothers, George and Amel, planted forbs and grasses for their livestock and those plants competed with the violet. The grasses break down less quickly than the native plants, leaving an accumulation of thatch that suffocates the violet's habitat. Other species took hold as well. Over-harvesting of elk removed Nature's mower from the scene. Just about everything humans have done along the coast has had an adverse effect on the insects, their food, and their mating activities. Construction of homes and businesses, traffic, logging, and recreational activities, disturb the violets' ability to grow and compromise the butterfly's ability to lay eggs, survive the caterpillar phase, and find shelter and mates in the forest.

A study conducted by students at Lewis & Clark College in Portland showed that a high concentration of violets is needed for the caterpillar to successfully complete that stage of its life cycle. Students marked the tiny caterpillars with a pink dye. They put a pin in the ground every thirty seconds to track the caterpillars' progress. What the study demonstrated is that not only do the caterpillars not move far, but they also move randomly and can't determine if they're moving toward a meal of violet leaves or toward some other plant that is of no use to them at all. The tedious lab work helped show why Silverspot populations were crashing and what was needed for them to recover.[43]

"Extirpated" is a chilling word meaning totally destroyed, exterminated, pulled out by the roots, and done away with. By the mid-1970s, the Silverspot was described as "extirpated"[44] from eleven localities, and the numbers at the remaining sites were at critical levels. In 1975, the U.S. Fish and Wildlife Service included the Oregon Silverspot in a status review, seeking information as to whether the insect should be proposed for listing as an Endangered or Threatened species. The factors jeopardizing the Silverspot's existence were threats to critical habitat from increased residential development and recreational activities along the coast. The area to be designated as Critical Habitat was in the northwest corner of Lane County and included the salt-spray meadows located in the four miles between Rock Creek on the north and Big Creek on the south. U.S. Highway 101 traversed the habitat area. On the east side of the highway were additional habitat sites and the western edge of the spruce forest that the butterflies used for shelter during their mating season in late August. Most of the land was already under federal ownership as part of the Siuslaw National Forest. There was a National Forest campground at Rock Creek, with access to the beach at the mouth. The affected area at Big Creek was mostly under private ownership.

After a delay due to 1978 amendments to the Endangered Species Act, the listing and Critical Habitat designation were re-proposed in March 1980. Oregon Governor Victor Atiyeh was notified as required. He supported listing the butterfly and designation of its critical habitat. Other agencies and interested parties were notified and invited to comment. A public meeting was held on April 15, 1980, and a public hearing was held on April 29, both in Newport, Oregon.

As expected, the proposal was supported by conservation organizations, including the Xerces Society and the International Union for Conservation of Nature and Natural Resources. Dr. Frederick Rindge, Curator of Lepidoptera at the American Museum of Natural History, supported the designation of Critical Habitat, but opposed listing because, he said, the distribution of the subspecies was uncertain. However, "Critical Habitat can only be designated in relation to a listed species," so it was necessary to list the Silverspot in order to protect its habitat—it occurs only on these coastal areas.[45]

One of the private landowners in the area was Hugh Sherwood who, with his wife Marguerite, owned 186 acres on the north and south sides of Big Creek, extending to and including the salt-spray meadows between the highway and the ocean. He had a potential buyer for the property—Victor Renaghan—who planned to build a resort there. Sherwood feared the listing of the Silverspot would prevent the type of development planned by Renaghan and would thus jeopardize the sale, or at the least cause the sale price to drop.[46]

In the end, the U.S. Fish and Wildlife Service did not include the Tenmile Creek area. In the Rock Creek/Big Creek area, the U.S. Fish & Wildlife Service accepted the Forest Service recommendation to move the eastern edge of the Critical Habitat area 1,500 feet to the west. The Service didn't believe Renaghan's development plans would have an adverse effect on butterfly habitat because there were already "considerable constraints" to development in the existing Lane County zoning designations, which restricted the property to timber harvest and wildlife preservation.[47]

The Director of the U.S. Fish & Wildlife Service determined "the Oregon Silverspot Butterfly is in danger of becoming extinct throughout all of its range." The Silverspot met two of the five criteria for listing: "present or threatened destruction, modification, or curtailment of its habitat or range," and "the inadequacy of existing regulatory mechanism." The Silverspot was listed as Threatened with Critical Habitat in those "portions of Lane County where a viable population of the butterfly is known to occur."[48]

The U.S. Fish & Wildlife Service and the Siuslaw National Forest Waldport Ranger Station began developing recovery plans that would protect and manage habitat, monitor the population of *Speyeria zerene*, and reduce take. "Take" is the term used in the Endangered Species Act to refer to any action that might harm a listed species directly or through significant habitat modification. A permit may be issued in which the applicant agrees to take measures that reduce or offset potential harms.

Victor Renaghan was undeterred by the potential problems of having a listed species on his property. He and his wife proceeded with their plan to develop a resort at the mouth of Big Creek. Along with another couple, they purchased the 186 acres owned by Hugh Sherwood and filed an application with Lane County for a zone change.

Vic Renaghan expressed good intentions toward *Speyeria zerene:* "These are my butterflies," he said at a meeting with the arbitrator regarding his plans to build a caretaker's cottage.[49] He repeatedly expressed his intent to make sure the butterflies, the elk, and the fish on his property would thrive.

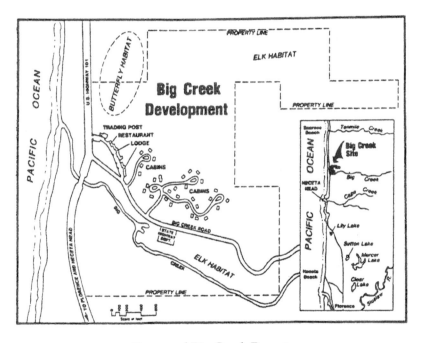

Proposed Big Creek Resort
(Source: "Pro and Con," *Oregon Coast Magazine*)

CHAPTER EIGHT
THE WEST LANE PLANNING COMMISSION

The zoning originally placed on this property was not erroneous.
—Steve May, West Lane Planning Commissioner

The West Lane County Planning Commission met in Florence, a once-booming lumber town near the mouth of the Siuslaw River, about twelve miles south of the Big Creek property. The hearings room was in a complex of one-story buildings with covered walkways between the rooms. It was paneled in dark wood, with the eight Commissioners seated in front, and the staff arranged at tables in front of them.

Hearings were held in the evening, on the second Wednesday of the month. In 1997, the West Lane hearings were merged into the regular Planning Commission hearings held in Eugene, but at the time of the Renaghan petition, the Florence location was still in use. On February 11, 1981, when Renaghan's request came up for the first time, Lane County planning staff Chris Crook, Jim Mann, and Michael Copely drove over from Eugene to present reports and provide technical support on land use law. They were prepared to explain how the zone change would be impacted by existing state and federal law and the county's own plans and procedures. Bill

Van Vactor, the county attorney, was also present.

Victor Renaghan is a man of strong opinions and self-confidence. He was ready to address any land use issues that might come up. In fact, he surmised that he and his planning staff were probably "too well prepared," overloading the Commission members with "economic impact studies, and reports on the relationship between the elk herd and my proposed development. We literally swamped them with facts and figures," he told Mary Lou Brown, who wrote an article about the resort controversy in *Oregon Coast Magazine*.[50]

Renaghan had no doubts. His development would be good for the coast economy and good for the environment too. "Land needs to be nurtured," he told Brown. "You can't leave all those acres of untended land unattended that close to the highway."[51]

Vic Renaghan's property was within the county's Coastal Area Sub-plan. Lane County's new Comprehensive Plan, designed to meet the state's land use requirements under Senate Bill 100, had not yet been approved by the Department of Land Conservation and Development. Nonetheless, the county was required to comply with the Statewide Planning Goals and Guidelines. Of particular relevance were Goal 4, intended to maintain forestlands for timber production, and Goal 17, which applied to the coastal shorelands and was particularly concerned with wildlife habitat protection.[52]

~

As with all land use issues, the heart of the conflict over the Big Creek Resort was who (or what) should use the land. State and local land use laws are based on the principle that society has a stake in how that question is answered. The 186 acres that the Renaghans had purchased, where they planned to build a resort facility with a lodge, restaurant, store, and cabins, had the cumbersome-sounding zone designation of "natural resource/timber/prime wildlife combining." That meant that Vic Renaghan could harvest the timber, but he couldn't build a resort. The prime wildlife overlay meant that this was wildlife habitat and should be preserved as such. Preserving wildlife habitat was not considered incompatible with logging.

Renaghan didn't have a problem with the wildlife designation. He was requesting a zone change to "tourist/commercial" for the northwest corner of the property where the resort would be built, and an amendment to the county's comprehensive plan to reflect the changed zoning. The rest of the property would be designated conservation/recreation/open space/ prime wildlife combining. He had no intention of logging the property, he said.[53]

The Renaghans did not waste any time in lining up arguments to support their petition. They engaged Michael Yeager, a planning consultant with the Eugene firm of David J. Peterson and Associates, and Michael Farthing, a land use attorney with Butler, Husk, Gleves & Swearingen, also from Eugene. Yeager immediately requested a Shorelands Boundary Review for the property. The review was conducted by Chris Crook, Coastal Planner for Lane County. It was not favorable to the Renaghans' petition.

Although the development would occur only on the thirty-five acres (reduced to twenty-six in the final plan) that the Renaghans wanted re-zoned to tourist commercial, Chris Crook pointed out that the three sensitive species on the property—elk, salmon, and Silverspot Butterfly—didn't restrict themselves to the kinds of boundaries that humans devised. "These species," she wrote, "do not necessarily share common habitat boundaries or experience the same reaction to human disturbance."[54]

Indeed they don't. Elk are large animals. They use all of the Big Creek site—the forested uplands, open meadows, clear-cuts, and wetlands. They go into the ocean to wash off parasites. They browse on the salt spray meadow vegetation, where their foraging controls the encroachment of plants that compete with the violets on which the Oregon Silverspot Butterfly larvae feed.

Elk "do not mix well with the level of human occupancy proposed for the site," according to the various agencies concerned with their well-being. Although they could be expected to avoid the area of human habitation, a few elk might wander onto the resort grounds and munch the landscape, which would "result in upsetting visitor interactions and hazard from hunters," who presumably would be invited to remove the thousand-pound pests and might accidentally shoot a guest at the lodge.[55]

Fish habitat, on the other hand, "is pretty much confined to Big Creek and its estuary," according to Crook's report. She mentions possible pollution from septic fields or sewage outfalls, ground disturbance during construction, and overfishing of the already depleted population of Coho salmon.[56]

The butterflies fell between the omnipresent elk and the restricted watery world of the fish. Silverspots lay their eggs on the salt spray meadows. Resort guests, exploring the meadows or crossing them to access the beach, would damage eggs and the plants that support butterfly larvae and adults. Adults shelter in nearby forested areas to escape wind and fog close to the shore. In the space between, courtship and mating take place.

All the habitat areas would be affected by different aspects of the resort development, from construction noise and disturbance to intrusions by overnight guests. Increased fishing pressure could be anticipated, beyond what the small wild runs on Big Creek could tolerate.

The Silverspot butterflies, which by this time had disappeared from all but two of their fifteen former sites in Oregon, were listed by the Environmental Protection Agency as Threatened. Opinions differed about the impact of the resort on their various habitat areas. Dr. Dave McCorkle, who had been one of the scientists responsible for getting the butterfly listed, testified that the larval breeding ground—the salt spray meadows—would not be threatened by the resort development. However, he was concerned about the possible application of spray against mosquitoes.[57] Other biologists, however, claimed that the butterfly population would be decimated by any increased activity on the salt spray meadows, as well as any obstacles in the way of finding shelter in the forest. Construction, landscaping, and herbicide spraying all would have negative effects.[58]

Crook's report supported the continued prime wildlife designation for the entire property. However, if the zoning were changed and plans to build the resort moved forward, she said, actions would need to be taken to protect the habitat under the requirements of Statewide Goal 17.[59]

U.S. Fish and Wildlife cautiously expressed an opinion in a letter to Michael Copely, the Lane County Planning Director, on January 22, 1981. Most of the planned resort development was within the Critical Habitat established when the Oregon Silverspot was listed under the Endangered Species Act. Joseph Blum, Area Manager for U.S. Fish & Wildlife, stated, "We firmly believe that Mr. Renaghan's proposed development is carefully thought out and would be carried out in an environmentally sensitive way." Nonetheless, "...the best interest of the Oregon Silverspot Butterfly would be served in not encouraging more human use on its habitat."[60]

The resort proponents disagreed that the resort would have a serious impact. "We're not attempting to locate Salishan [a large destination resort with residential development near Lincoln City, Oregon] on Big Creek," Michael Yeager, the planner, testified. Besides, he claimed, "400,000 tourists visit this area yearly," and the resort wouldn't add much to that number.[61]

Additional testimony about the negative effect of the resort on wildlife was presented by Jerry MacLeod, Siuslaw District Fish

Biologist for the Oregon Department of Fish and Wildlife (ODFW). At the hearing on February 11, he spoke primarily about the fish population in Big Creek.

Natural fish populations inhabiting Big Creek include winter steelhead, Coho salmon, sea-run trout, and resident cutthroat trout. The stream was managed for wild fish, which means it wasn't managed; no hatchery fish were released into the stream. Compared with bigger, more accessible rivers like the Siuslaw to the south or the Alsea to the north, there were few anglers on Big Creek.

Visitors staying at the lodge would undoubtedly be attracted to the banks of Big Creek to try their luck. More adult fish would be caught, reducing the number available for spawning. During the summer, anglers might fish for trout, but they'd end up catching the young salmon that hang around near the mouth of the creek before they migrate into the ocean.[62]

Jerry MacLeod wasn't reluctant to speak his mind about the zone change request. "This is precisely the type of land use change that land use planning was intended to prevent—the expansion of 'satellite developments' in remote rural areas," he said. He wasn't charmed by the use of the word "cabins" to refer to what would be a 30-unit subdivision. "This is the kind of development that would completely change the nature of the area and threaten its continued use as wildlife habitat or timber production. It does not appear consistent with proper land use planning."[63]

He also asked where the two owners' residences—proposed in Renaghan's plan—would be built. If the intent was to build them outside the actual resort development, they would be in the Conservation/Recreation/Open Space zone, which was not intended to include a private residence.[64]

Vic Renaghan responded that he would never build in the Prime Wildlife zone, which meant anywhere outside the thirty-five acres to be approved for Tourist Commercial. Far from arguing against the staff reports detailing what actions would have to be taken under the statewide goals to protect wildlife, Renaghan appeared to be enthusiastic about maintaining good habitat for the animals on his property. He and his wife would hatch butterflies, he vowed, giving them a better survival rate than they had in the wild.[65] Renaghan later told a reporter that his wife had "adopted" the elk herd and that they planned to live on the property and protect the herd from harassment.[66]

In fact, according to both Mike Farthing, the lawyer, and Mike Yeager, the planner, the development would have a beneficial effect on wildlife in the area. The Renaghans would seal off the road leading to elk areas; no development would occur in the estuary; and the planned development would not affect the stream. There would be no further logging once the development site was cleared. Yeager also noted that not using the land "would not enhance the elk habitat."[67]

All proponents of timber harvest state that elk forage in clear-cuts. This, of course, is true only after something to forage appears—either trees planted by the logging company, or natural reproduction of alder, huckleberry, and other shrubs that elk browse. The same thing happens following a forest fire. Elk hunters often train their binoculars on clear-cuts.

~

When Oregon's revolutionary land use planning law, Senate Bill 100, was first proposed, its main objectives were to protect the twin pillars of Oregon's economy—agriculture and timber. Just as prime farmland was threatened by urban sprawl, prime timber production was threatened by recreational developments. Statewide Goal 4 was adopted to make sure there would be an adequate supply of harvestable trees.

Foresters worried that the endless forest would turn into endless acres of forest resorts or, closer to urban areas, conversions to housing developments and shopping malls. Between 1970 and 1977, the state lost an average of 175,000 acres of timberland every year. The loss was a new phenomenon: 99 percent of timberlands lost in the previous twenty-five years occurred during the 1970s.[68]

The Coast Range of Oregon is one of the best tree-growing environments in the world, but harvests were low in the early days of Euro-American settlement because there were no roads to transport logs to markets. Most of the timber was used locally. Trees were felled using axes and the two-man crosscut saw, sometimes called the "misery whip," although a Forest Service crosscut saw manual claims that until very recently, a crosscut could hold its own against a chainsaw. One bucker set a record of one minute, twenty-six and two-fifths seconds to buck (cut a downed tree into manageable lengths) a 32-inch diameter Douglas-fir log. But felling the old growth giants was another matter. The trees of the virgin forests of the Pacific Northwest were huge, topped only by the coast redwood in northern California. A height of 197 to 246 feet wasn't uncommon, with a base diameter of 4.9 to 6.6 feet. Specimens have been documented as high as 390 feet and as wide at the base as 20 feet.[69]

After World War II, harvest volumes increased dramatically. Harvest technology and transportation improved, and demand grew as the economy expanded. In 1943, 37.2 MMBF (million board feet) came off the Siuslaw National Forest. The volume increased steadily, to an astonishing peak of 461.4 MMBF in 1964. Additional harvest came off privately owned industrial forestlands.[70]

Oregon State University's Department of Forestry prepared a report, "Factors Affecting Land Use Planning Decisions on Forest Land," which was submitted in support of continuing the timber zoning of the Renaghan property. The concerns in the OSU report were not just about removing trees in order to develop a resort, but also the use conflicts that were sure to arise.

Fire was probably the most troubling. The fearsome image of kids playing with matches was raised in the report. Residential roads created hazards for the big fire-fighting equipment that would be brought in if there were a forest fire. Evacuation operations would complicate efforts to control the fire. And, as the Forest Service and other forestry operations were beginning to discover, people in residential areas were starting to notice—and object to—such essential management tools as herbicide spraying. This resulted in a broad buffer being needed between the forest and the residential areas, which meant more forestland taken out of timber production.[71]

The Oregon State report was, therefore, favorable to the state's land use planning decision articulated in Goal 4, to "preserve and protect... the supply of raw forest products and insure the stability" of rural counties. The economic benefits that might be generated from resort development in Lane County were negligible compared to the revenues and payroll produced by the timber industry, according to the report.[72]

The proponents of the Big Creek Resort claimed there would be little impact on timber production from their project. Although the natural resource/timber designation applied to the entire property, Renaghan claimed there was no commercial timber value on the northwest corner where the resort would be built. The spruce trees, Renaghan said, "were deformed and buffeted by high winds and salt spray." However, he also said he had no plans for logging "there or anywhere else on the property."[73]

~

Several local residents showed up at the first hearing on the Renaghan petition. Chuck Hoaks, a steelhead fisherman from

Florence, was concerned that the resort would attract more people to the creek, putting too much pressure on the fish population. Eric Twombly, who lived on the North Fork Siuslaw Road that meets Big Creek Road at the top of the ridge, said he was against increased development in the area. Another Florence resident, Robert Manseth, protested that the proponents of the resort development had not offered any drawings to show what the resort would look like, which he said was "like offering a blank check for signature."[74]

The West Lane Planning Commission received a stack of letters, almost all of them expressing opposition to the resort and any change to the zoning of the property. Letters were neatly typed under official letterhead, printed on lined paper, or scrawled in undecipherable pencil. The Survival Center at the University of Oregon sent two formal analyses of the impact a resort development would have on the site. Friends of the Umpqua objected, as did the Oregon Shores Conservation Coalition, representing 500 members. There was even a letter from Elizabeth Bond Starker, owner of a strip of beach property immediately west of the Renaghans' property, who suggested that if the zoning was changed on the Renaghans' property, hers should also be re-zoned to allow commercial development. She didn't indicate what sort of development, if any, she had in mind.

Al Wysong, the Planning Commission chair, proposed that the matter be taken up at the next meeting, on March 11, 1981, to give the Commissioners time to study all of the material that had been presented regarding the zone change. Additional written testimony could be submitted up to two weeks prior to the meeting on March 11; no oral testimony would be taken at the next hearing. Fred Jensen seconded the motion. It was approved unanimously.[75]

On March 11, the audio system wasn't working in the Planning Commission meeting room. "Anyone offering testimony," announced Chairman Wysong, "needs to speak loudly." In regard to the Renaghan petition, volume was not an issue. Both sides agreed to postpone any decision on the zone change to the next meeting of the Planning Commission, on April 8.[76]

Tony Cole arrived promptly at 7:30 p.m. on April 8, and took a seat in the back of the room. His wife, Ginger, who had left the Big Creek property and moved to Florence, also attended the hearing. Closer to the front, Vic Renaghan sat flanked by Mike Yeager, his planning consultant, and Mike Farthing, his land use attorney. Yeager spoke first, urging the Planning Commission to approve his client's request in a resolution that would establish guarantees to insure that objectives concerning wildlife were met.

"Mr. and Mrs. Renaghan fully intend to cooperate with the relevant agencies. They are committed to protecting the wildlife on their property," he stated. He also pointed out that he had analyzed alternative sites for the resort and concluded that there were no other suitable sites in Lane County.[77]

Dr. Robert Vincent, the Renaghans' wildlife consultant, testified that he had visited the Big Creek site earlier in the day. He knew the property well, having visited it frequently over the past forty years, doing a field reconnaissance in 1978 and a helicopter reconnaissance the following year. He could foresee problems with the elk harassing people at the resort, and vice versa, but he didn't see any problem with the fishery in Big Creek because the spawning grounds were above the development. In any case, he said, fishing shouldn't be regulated through zoning.[78]

Tony Cole was recognized and stepped forward to address the Commissioners. Wearing a plaid shirt with rolled up sleeves over a turtleneck, he didn't look like a wild hippie, as he had occasionally been characterized by the resort supporters. "My name is Tony Cole, and I live six miles up Big Creek Road," he stated. He was opposed to the Renaghans' plans for a resort at Big Creek. "It's not the Planning Commission's obligation" he said, "to provide transient populations with overnight accommodations." There was no reason to change the zone to permit development on one of the few remaining undeveloped areas of the central coast.[79]

Ginger Cole told the Commissioners that the meadows where the butterflies lay their eggs would be destroyed by building a resort in such close proximity. She didn't believe that the Renaghans' plan to build greenhouses and assist in hatching Silverspot eggs would do much to help the butterflies.[80]

Although Tom Smith didn't attend this hearing, he had provided Tony with information about the habitat needs of the butterfly. When Tony spoke again, he pointed out that the butterflies used more of the site than just the salt spray meadows. "They fly into the forest to get out of the wind and the fog," he said. "If the resort is built, they'd have to fly across the inhabited area to seek shelter." The already decimated population was bound to be harmed.[81]

There was another person at the meeting to speak against the zone change, someone neither Tony nor Ginger had met before. Tom Smith probably had met Bob Warren at a meeting of the Oregon Wilderness Coalition and suggested he attend the hearing. Bob was known as an outspoken, passionate environmental activist. He had worked with the Sierra Club, successfully blocking plans to build a new runway for the Coos Bay airport, which would have extended into the bay and caused environmental harm. He worked as a seasonal employee for the Forest Service, living with his wife, Mary Maggs Warren, on Siltcoos Lake just south of Florence.[82]

Bob Warren considered himself an "environmental mercenary."[83] He was young and arrogant, although he eschewed the radical hippie look for a buttoned-down appearance. In the future, he would work on environmental issues for Congressman Peter DeFazio and later for Governor Barbara Roberts. Like so many others, he gave credit to Tom Smith for teaching him how to be more effective in fighting for the environment. At the West Lane hearing, however, he didn't hold back. After submitting written testimony from the Oregon Wilderness Coalition, Warren angrily told the Commissioners that no resort was needed at Big Creek and there was no need to change the zone designation

"Just because this developer has a lot of money and is willing to go to extremes to get approval, means he clearly expects to reap a lot from his investment," he said. It would be wrong to sacrifice the wild undeveloped character of the site so that somebody could make a lot of money. "The best way to protect this property," Warren concluded, "is to leave it alone."[84]

~

Besides providing a convenient venue where local planning issues could be heard, the West Lane Planning Commission represented coastal interests and expertise. There was an assumption that the eight people on the Commission were more familiar with their part of the world than the Planning Commission in Eugene, and could bring that knowledge to bear on issues that pertained to the coastal part of Lane County. Goal 2 in the Statewide Goals calls for "an adequate factual basis to be the foundation of all decisions relating to use of land."[85] In the county planning department analysis of how Lane County would implement the Statewide Goals, specific reference was made to the county's two Planning Commissions: "The West Lane Planning Commission covers the western part of the County. This coastal area has a great deal of geographically unique features that the West Lane Planning Commission, because of their time, effort and familiarity with the area, have developed a great amount of expertise with, and which they bring to the quasi-judicial land use process."[86] As they approached a decision on the Renaghans' request for a zone change at Big Creek, the Commissioners relied on this unique perspective.

One factor they were certainly familiar with was the economy. A year-end summary of important news of 1981 reported on the impact of state and federal budget cuts, high interest rates that slowed new home starts, and layoffs in the timber industry.[87] As timber and fishing jobs disappeared, the coast economy withered. The difference was not made up through tourism. Tourism revenues on the central and south part of the Oregon Coast lagged behind the north coast, which was less than a two-hour drive from Portland. Even then, tourism jobs were mostly low paying and seasonal. It would be another decade before the influx of retirees began to change the coastal economy.

Commissioner Shirley Gardinier reminded the Commissioners to be mindful of the need for economic opportunities on the coast. She said that Statewide Goal 9 required communities to make sure they provided adequate opportunities for economic growth in drawing up their comprehensive plans, adding that there were other issues to take into consideration, including selecting areas where growth was compatible with the surrounding area and avoiding unplanned sprawl in sensitive areas. The Commission should make sure there was adequate infrastructure support, a supply of workers, and whatever other resources and materials would be needed. "We must take this into consideration when we make our decision," she concluded.[88]

Commissioner Donna Shelton said bluntly, "This is the wrong proposal for this site." She cited Goal 1: Citizen Involvement. Local residents opposed to the plan had taken the time to attend the meetings and speak up for their right to "live here and enjoy the land as it is."[89] Their views should be strongly considered.

Four criteria were listed in the county's code dealing with plan amendments. Any one of the four criteria would suffice to justify a recommendation to amend the county's land use plan. The criteria were: an error in the plan; changed circumstances affecting or pertaining to the plan; a change in public policy; or a change in public need based on a re-evaluation of the factors affecting the plan.

"Mr. Renaghan's plan has not met any of the criteria," said Commission Chair Steve May. "The zoning originally placed on this property was not erroneous."[90]

May moved that the plan amendment be denied. Donna Shelton seconded, and the motion passed unanimously. May then moved that the request for a zone change also be denied. Fred Jensen seconded, and again the vote was unanimous. Michael Copely, the planning director, stated that the resolution for the amendment to the county's comprehensive plan, which the West Lane Planning Commissioner had just denied, would go before the Board of Commissioners if it were appealed.[91]

Tom Smith and the rest of the resort opponents breathed a sigh of relief. Without the zone change, Vic Renaghan's dream of a destination resort at Big Creek was over.

CHAPTER NINE
EARLY SETTLEMENT

Just as the Renaghans' development wasn't the first resort proposed for Big Creek, Tom Smith and the community of back-to-the-land counterculture residents of the 1970s weren't the first people to be attracted to this area of stunning landscape and bountiful resources.

The same geologic forces that made Big Creek unsuitable for locating a nuclear power plant also make it difficult to have certain knowledge about the people who lived in this area before Euro-Americans arrived. The land rose and fell; glaciers melted and sea levels rose. Some formerly inhabited areas along the coast, particularly the central part where Big Creek is located, are now three miles west of the current shore, and the villages that once existed there have disappeared under the ocean.

There is disagreement about who came, and when they came, and how many different groups arrived, but the consensus is that by 14,000 years ago, humans had settled in the Western Hemisphere, leaving evidence of habitation as far south as Chile.[92]

University of Oregon archaeologist Jon Erlandson believes people followed the "kelp highway,"[93] a generous provender of fish and marine mammals extending along the coasts from Asia to the

Americas. Evidence found on the Channel Islands (offshore from Santa Barbara, California) indicates that humans inhabited the north island 13,000 years ago. They would have needed boats to cross the five miles of open water between the island and the mainland, so it's not too far-fetched to think that boats were used to explore along the coast.

There is no evidence for such early settlement at Big Creek, although to the north and south, where the land has risen rather than subsided, settlements have been dated back to 12,000 years ago. At Big Creek, there are shell middens—garbage dumps that are a rich source of information about the diet of early inhabitants—and a Paleolithic house pit. The most reliable dates for the site, like others on this part of the coast, are between 1,500 and 3,000 years ago according to Phyllis Steeves, former Archaeologist on the Siuslaw National Forest.[94]

Big Creek was used seasonally by the Siuslaw Indians, whose main villages were to the south. The Alsea people to the north also visited the area, with Tenmile Creek being the most likely boundary between the territories of the two tribes.[95] Boundaries were not rigid. Don Whereat, who was a tribal elder of the Confederated Tribes of Coos, Lower Umpqua, and Siuslaw Indians, told Steeves that it was acceptable for a hunter in pursuit of an elk to cross into another tribe's territory, but it was not okay to begin a hunt there.[96] Resources were plentiful, however, and there doesn't appear to have been a lot of jostling for territory.

Jesse Beers, Culture Director of the Confederated Tribes, thinks there may have been more mingling, though the tribes to the north spoke Athabascan languages while those to the south spoke Penutian languages.[97]

The ocean provided fat-rich seals and sea lions, the occasional whale that washed up on the beach, many varieties of fin fish, and of course salmon, which conveniently presented themselves by swimming up the coastal rivers and creeks to spawn, an occurrence arranged for the People by Coyote the Trickster, told in myths shared by many of the northwest tribes.

The intertidal areas were a banquet table of clams, mussels, whelks, rock oysters, black-katy chitons, and seaweed. Large flocks of ducks and geese settled on the bays and estuaries. Oregon grape (*Mahonia aquifolium*), huckleberry, salmonberry, wild strawberries, and the low-growing native blackberries were gathered and dried. The dark purple, almost black, berries of the omnipresent salal (*Gaultheria shallon*) were used as a dye and as medicine to treat coughs, skin conditions, and stomach problems. Elk, deer, bear and other mammals were hunted, their meat dried and stored for winter. Cedar for constructing canoes and for building plank houses, and all the reeds and grasses, roots and shoots necessary for clothing, baskets, and other utensils were available. The tribes moved around according to the season. It was a good life and it lasted a long, long time.

~

Europeans reached the Pacific Northwest in the sixteenth century. The Spanish explorer Juan Rodriguez Cabrillo sailed along the Oregon Coast in 1543. Juan de Fuca made detailed maps on his voyage of 1592. Seeking to secure its claim to the fur-rich Pacific Northwest, Spain authorized routine explorations starting in 1774, but the British also had their eye on the prize—James Cook sailed east from Hawai'i in 1778, making landfall at a point he named Cape Foulweather, north of present day Newport, Oregon. He sailed south and then north again, mapping, trading for sea otter pelts, and trying to find the Northwest Passage. He then went back across the Pacific to Hawai'i where he was killed by the local people.

The young United States of America, having purchased a vast territory from France, sent Meriwether Lewis and James Clark to survey and study their new acquisition. In 1805-06, Lewis and Clark's Corps of Discovery built Fort Clatsop south of the mouth of the Columbia River as their winter encampment. James Jacob Astor built his fur depot there in 1811. After that, the destruction of the Native way of life moved forward with inexorable speed.

In July 1826, trappers from the Hudson's Bay Company reached the Siuslaw River. Jedediah Smith and his party came into the country along the lower Umpqua River two years later. Methodist missionaries arrived in 1840 with the intent of establishing a mission among the Indians. They found only two hundred people living in the area in three small villages.

After contact with Euro-Americans, the populations of Native people had plummeted. The Indians had no immunity to diseases carried by the newcomers. Smallpox, transmitted by sailors on merchant ships, killed nine out of ten people along the North Coast. It didn't require open warfare to overcome the Native people, although there were some violent clashes between Indians and the increasing numbers of settlers, trappers, and miners possessed by gold fever.

The Coos and Lower Umpqua villagers were peaceful, but that was not true of all Indians along the coastal rivers. The pressure on the land and its resources ramped up as settlers followed the Oregon Trail into the Willamette Valley and gradually penetrated the valleys leading to the coast. At the same time, gold miners pressed up from northern California. The resources on which the Native people's existence depended — game, wood, clean water — disappeared.[98]

On October 31, 1855, a force of Army dragoons, militiamen, and three hundred local volunteers attacked two hundred Native warriors above a steep ravine located in the rough terrain between the Umpqua and Rogue drainages. The Americans were at a strategic disadvantage. The Indians, with musket and bow-and-arrow, picked them off as they charged up the hill. The Indians won this particular battle in what was known as the Rogue River War, but the outcome of the larger struggle was never in doubt. Defeated, the Native people were eventually rounded up and sent to Oregon reservations at Grande Ronde and Siletz.

Meanwhile, policy toward the other coast tribes was mixed. The coast tribes were the last of the Indians in Oregon to be "treatied," just as the central coast was the last area to be settled by Euro-Americans. Compared to the Eden of the Willamette Valley, the coast offered little to attract settlers, and the government didn't figure they were giving much away when they created the large Coast Reservation for the Indians. As the Rogue River War spread to the coast south of the Umpqua, members of the Lower Umpqua and Coos Tribes were moved to Fort Umpqua, allegedly for their own safety.

By 1857, there were about seven hundred people confined to the fort at Umpqua City. As the hostile tribes were pacified, the Umpqua people began to grow restless. The hostile Indians received supplies and annuities according to the terms of the treaty that ended the Rogue War, but the Coos and Lower Umpqua received nothing, in spite of having signed a treaty (which was never ratified). By the end of the decade, the Army concluded it could no longer "protect" the Indians. In fact, the number of soldiers assigned to the area was being drawn down as the country moved closer to civil war.

In 1859, members of the Coos and Lower Umpqua tribes were removed north to a reservation near the present town of Yachats. The forced march was brutal. The Army pushed them on a trail of tears and blood along the sharp lava rocks, through thickets of salal and bracken, over headlands and along the beaches to the sub-agency at Yachats. A band of the Alsea people had lived along the river once, but had perished from disease.

The sub-agency was located on a barren windswept prairie where it was virtually impossible to grow crops. The Indians subsisted on mussels scraped from the rocks. Promised supplies were never delivered, the weather was harsh, and their treatment at the hands of George W. Collins, the Agent at the Yachats sub-agency, was even harsher. Many people died and a short time later, less than half of the original group was left. Gradually, a few survivors managed to clear land along the Yachats River and began to grow some food. At that point, the reservation was opened to white settlement and the Native people were pushed out to make their way as best they could either north to the Siletz Reservation or south, back to the Umpqua where the home they once had was gone. Death and despair were associated with Yachats to such an extent that members of the Confederated Tribes of Coos, Lower Umpqua, and Siuslaw Indians wouldn't set foot in the area until the end of the twentieth century when the efforts of several Yachats residents to acknowledge and publicize the crimes that had been committed began a healing process.[99]

The one million acres of the Coast Reservation were reduced piecemeal by several Acts of Congress until the Dawes Act of 1892 finally terminated what remained. The Indians received 160-acre allotments and were paid $142,600 for the unallocated portion, which happened to be "covered with some of the finest timber in the world." In 1907, Stephen A.D. Puter, in his book, *Looters of the Public Domain*, estimated the value of the property at about $8 million.[100]

CHAPTER TEN
HOMESTEADERS

The coast offered immigrants an excellent opportunity for survival,
but a poor outlook for prosperity

— Ward Tonsfeldt, *Celebrating the Siuslaw*

...the original Ten Milers no longer living would like knowing that
some part of history important to them is recorded.

— Mary F. Beck, *The Ten Mile Story*

When the good land in the Willamette Valley was gone, homesteaders found their way over the Coast Range to claim land. The government required settlers to "prove up" their claim, meaning make improvements—build a place to live, plant crops, raise animals. After the Siuslaw National Forest was formed in 1908, there was a two-year window for people to claim land within the Forest better suited to agriculture than forestry, under the Forest Homestead Act of June 11, 1906. Settlement was closed between 1910 and 1913, opened again for three years, then closed permanently. During this time, 1,115 forest homestead claims were filed. Some were fraudulent, but many represented a real desire to obtain good homestead land in the National Forest before it was gone.[101]

The Euro-Americans who came to settle along this part of the coast were generally looking for land to farm. Along the small ocean tribs—heavily forested slopes and narrow valleys—the land was less desirable than parcels along the Alsea River or the Yachats River. Except for the land around the mouth, Big Creek was one of the less attractive locations, since the creek cut a narrow channel through the mountains, with only a few benches flat enough to farm.

The same was true of Tenmile Creek, though the canyon was a little wider and there was more land that could support a homestead. Nonetheless, eventually claims were made even on these marginal lands.

In the Siuslaw National Forest collection of photos of homesteaders,[102] an old photograph shows five people leading their pack animals along a trail that has been hacked out of the forest. Branches had been chopped down to clear the track, then laid along the downhill side and filled in with dirt and rocks to create a path just wide enough for a mule. Canvas packs, bristling with tools and shovels, are roped to the mules' backs. I imagine the animals move slowly, seeking a sturdy foothold. Loose pebbles and dirt, dislodged by their hooves, rattle down to the creek.

There is an older man, two adult sons, a young boy, and a young woman. She might be a daughter, or the wife of one of the sons. She is slim and attractive, but hard looking. Her dark hair is pulled back under a leather slouch-brimmed hat and she wears a skirt and jacket in a tailored, military style that look, in the black and white photo, as if they might be a dull olive. A rifle is slung across her shoulder.

Where the slope is too precipitous, or the ground too hard for the trail, the family would have led the mules down to the creek, splashing through, crossing from one side to the other, the animals picking their way carefully among the rocks and cobbles. Perhaps they head up another smaller creek where they've carved out a trail of switchbacks along the steep side of the canyon. They arrive at their homestead, tired, cold, and probably wet. Perhaps there is an older woman waiting for them, with two or three small children, a kettle of soup simmering on the hob. Perhaps she waited anxiously, anticipating their arrival, standing in front of the tanned deer hide that served as a door.

Who are these people? On which creek is their dark, primitive cabin? What year is it? What became of them? Very likely, they were bought out by the federal government during the Depression, if they lasted that long. Or the Forest Service ranger may have finally made his way to their homestead, leading a pack mule up the same trail, to determine if their claim met the criteria of the June 11 Act. It's possible too that they didn't have a claim, that they had just a summer camp for hunting and trapping, berry picking, and collecting cascara bark.

According to Ward Tonsfeldt, who wrote *Celebrating the Siuslaw* to commemorate the one-hundredth anniversary of the Siuslaw National Forest, homesteaders lived a marginal existence, a constant struggle to keep the vegetation cleared, to provide food for the family, to earn enough cash to pay their taxes. There were no roads. People hacked their way through the dense salal and blackberry vines or came down the larger rivers and then made their way along the shore, using the beach as a roadway where possible at low tide, building crude ferries across the Yaquina, the Alsea, and the Siuslaw rivers.[103]

The homesteaders might have had a cow or a few goats, maybe some chickens. They could hunt for game—at least until elk hunting was restricted because they'd been hunted out of existence. In many families, the father or older sons found seasonal work as loggers or on fishing boats, later on construction projects like the Coast Highway. Even the women went to work, often at the canneries that lined the major ports, processing and canning salmon that fed poor people in industrial cities in the east.

Cascara was plentiful in the Coast Range. Also called chittum, the plant is a member of the buckthorn family and is used as a laxative. The bark was stubbed, or stripped, off the lower part of the tree, then the tree was cut down and the rest of the bark was removed. The dried bark sold for just ¾ of a cent per pound, but if a family could cut and dry a hundred pounds, they would have enough cash to buy coffee, sugar, and flour.[104]

Not all of the newly formed Siuslaw National Forest was surveyed before it was opened to homesteading. People made their claims and eventually a district ranger rode out to document if the homesteaders met the requirements. The ranger looked for tools, furniture, supplies, and livestock to indicate that the inhabitants really intended to stay and make this their home. The reports provide a grim picture of what it must have been like, trying to survive in the river valleys along the coast. One cabin consisted of a stable at one end and the family's residence at the other; the stable end was much the cleaner. This poor place had almost nothing—a Holy Bible, a stool, a half-empty bag of flour. No one was there. The homesteader had gone away to earn some cash or had given up.[105]

Even if they could grow something to sell, the homesteaders had no way—no efficient way—to get it to market. There were sawmills on most of the creeks, but until the major public investment in road building began during the Depression, there was no commercial value to those trees unless they were close to a creek. Held in a splash dam, the logs were carried by the rushing water to a larger river where they could be floated to a port for shipment to San Francisco. Otherwise, the timber had no value except for local use.

Many homesteaders lost their claims because they didn't have the cash to pay taxes on the property. Others settlers gobbled up the homesteads that were in arrears. Properties were bought by timber companies after road construction made it feasible to get the logs to market. During the Depression, the federal Resettlement Administration created the Western Oregon Scattered Settlers Project to buy out and re-settle many of the early homesteaders. Most of the old homesteads became part of the Siuslaw National Forest.

Stan Poe, who helped Tom Smith and his family when they first moved to Tenmile, told Tom and Billie Jo that he moved his family to Upper Tenmile Creek in the 1950s because he'd always wanted to live the way his homesteading ancestors had lived. In 1978, Hans Radtke, a more recent arrival to the community (and someone who would play an important part in saving Big Creek), videotaped an interview with Stan, then in his fifties. When asked how those early settlers made a living, Stan said, "They just lived. They didn't have the same expectations."

They raised what food they could, hunted and trapped, fished, kept dairy cows. The McKinney family, for example, one of the most remote of the early Tenmile homesteaders, couldn't grow much other than potatoes in the thin soil on their property, but they had some cows. "You got milk and potatoes?" said Poe. "Then you got potato soup."[106]

~

Calling the rough track along the coast a road was laughable, although it was no laughing matter to those early settlers if they misjudged the tides and got their wagons stuck in the sand. Using a lot of dynamite, some of the settlers eventually blasted a road around the headlands. Wagons maneuvered backward and forward to get around the tight curves. By the 1920s, it was possible to drive a car from Waldport to Tenmile. The mail was delivered in a motorized vehicle, but it was a slow, bone-shattering ride.[107]

The Stonefield brothers were among the more successful settlers along the Central Oregon Coast at the end of the 19th century. There were four, and they all had land claims in the area, on Tenmile Creek and on Big Creek. The most prominent of the brothers were George and Amel. They owned "all the land (north) from Big Creek to Bray's Point (about five miles) and east to Forest Service land." They put gates at both ends and ran cattle between the two properties.[108]

George lived at the mouth of Tenmile, in the house that was eventually bought by Tom and Billie Jo Smith. Amel lived at the mouth of Big Creek. Neither married until they were in their fifties. George married Mahala Baker, though the old-timers were puzzled by this act since she was already married to Jack Baker, George's friend. George, according to memoirs by old-timers in the area, was not the philandering type, but Mahala apparently was persuasive. Years later, she told one of the "city folk" who came to Tenmile for summer vacations that she climbed through George's bedroom window one night, and then Jack had to give her a divorce. Mahala and George stayed married until her death in the early 1940s. Jack and George worked together on various projects, but Jack would not come in the house to take a meal with Mr. and Mrs. G. Stonefield.[109]

Amel Stonefield's two-story house was just north of the mouth of Big Creek, near where Tom Smith saw the Big Creek Resort sign. Homesteaders further up the valley collected their mail there. Marie Linton, a thirty-nine year old divorced woman who had a homestead up Big Creek, passed Amel's house whenever she picked up her mail and she decided she was going to marry him. They married in 1920, when Amel was nearing sixty. In spite of the age difference, "people said she was a good wife for Amel."[110] She ran the Roosevelt Beach Post Office, at the mouth of Big Creek, from 1920 to 1940.[111] The Big Creek property that Vic Renaghan bought in 1980 came down through her.

John Thompson, a relative of Marie Linton Stonefield, moved to Waldport from California and applied for a homestead on Upper Big Creek. In 1916, he moved his family—his wife, Arvilla Jane McCollum, and two boys, Orvie, age six, and Cecil, a few years younger—to the new homestead. He transported everything they'd need on horses or on an "Indian wagon," which consisted of two long poles fastened to the horse's collar with a platform attached to the poles and loaded with the heavier items like beds and the stove. "With a slow and steady horse," Cecil Thompson remembered years later, "the load could be moved along the trail quite safely."[112] They lived in a vacant homestead two miles below their property while John built a neat log cabin "out of the woods," since there was no commercial lumber available.[113]

Like most of the families that settled along the coastal tribs, the Thompson family and their neighbors made improvements— clearing land, planting gardens and orchards, putting up outbuildings. They built a schoolhouse and hired a teacher, who boarded with the Thompsons. The community applied for county help to improve the road—they got some money and a little powder (dynamite)—and built a bridge across the creek so the kids wouldn't have to use a foot-log to cross the rapidly-flowing creek on their way to school. When the Thompsons traveled to Florence for supplies, they usually stopped at the cattle ranch of Aunt Marie and Uncle Amel Stonefield for a night. It was a three-day trip each way.

After completing ninth grade, the Thompson boys were enrolled at Benson Polytechnic High School in Portland. Eventually, most of the homesteaders sold out. Cecil returned in 1975 to hunt elk and found "Nothing but brush, with now and then an apple tree." He hoped that "someday another community will be planted," so that other children could have the same wonderful childhood he had.[114]

~

Not all the settlers were homesteaders. People were beginning to appreciate the beauty and recreational attractions of the Oregon Coast. In 1917, Mike Bauer, who was a tailor and owned a laundry and dry cleaning business in Corvallis, came out to the coast with some friends to hunt and fish. Later they brought their families.[115]

Mike Bauer and his wife Ednah camped with their family and friends on the ocean side of George Stonefield's property. They built primitive cabins there, and then more substantial cabins slightly inland and on the south side of the river, first leasing and eventually buying the property from "Uncle" George. In the years that followed, Bauer became a strong supporter of local improvements. He was one of the people who worked with George Stonefield and some dynamite to build the road around Cape Perpetua. He also promoted construction of the Alsea Highway, from Corvallis to Waldport.[116]

Ralph Beck, Ednah Bauer's half-brother, was a county agent based in Corvallis. He worked with the agriculture extension program at the state college. He got to know the coast—and George Stonefield—because he and his wife Ruth produced a radio show to teach homesteaders about farming, and how to preserve and cook food. Ruth had a brother, also a faculty member, who built a cabin at Tenmile. Known as "Little Corvallis," the community grew until there were quite a few cabins used by members of the extended families. Some of them eventually became year-round homes. The property is still in the family.[117]

Over the next few decades, parts of the original Stonefield properties were sold off. In January 1931, property that was jointly owned by Amel and Marie (sometimes called Mary) Stonefield, and George and Mahala Stonefield, was deeded to the State of Oregon as right of way for construction of Highway 101. In May 1934, the two brothers and their wives sold some of their property to the

Forest Service, and Amel and Marie sold additional acreage to the Forest Service, plus a strip of land sixty feet wide, starting at Highway 101, which became Big Creek Road, built with labor from the Civilian Conservation Corps unit stationed at Cape Perpetua. Tenmile Creek Road was also built at this time. Before that, there was only the creek bed and trails that the homesteaders made.

On the 14th of June 1963, Mary Stonefield, then a widow, sold lots 2, 3, and 4 in Section 15, Township 16 South, Range 12 West of the Willamette Meridian, to Bruce Starker for ten dollars and "and other good and valuable consideration." She retained a life estate in the property, with the right to live in her house at the mouth of Big Creek and to collect rents for grazing and for any other buildings on the property.[118]

The property then shifted to the Sherwoods. In 1968, a one-half interest in the property was conveyed by Marguerite Sherwood to her husband, Hugh Sherwood, Jr. for the "true and actual consideration… (of) love and affection."[119] The Sherwoods were still the owners in 1979 when Vic and Linda Renaghan negotiated an option to buy 186 acres. The option was exercised and the title transferred to the Renaghans on December 14, 1980, for $293,000.[120]

Chapter Eleven
SB 100: Oregon's Statewide
Land Use Law

...why the hell don't you just give me $500,000, and I'll zone the goddamn state?

—Tom McCall, Governor of Oregon 1966-1974

In the 1960s, Oregon was still mostly forests and farms. Portland was a stodgy city of brick canyons where the streetlights went on at midday in the winter, and it felt like winter most of the time. West of the Cascades was wet and gray. East of the Cascades was dry and empty. The sour smell of wigwam burners, which were used to dispose of waste from sawmills, filled the air. Industrial runoff polluted the Willamette River; fish floated belly up. People left the state if they wanted to get ahead.

Ten years later, things hadn't changed much. You could still rent a little house on an abandoned farm outside Eugene for sixty dollars a month, or a rambling Victorian in Portland, easily affordable when shared with friends. But change was coming.

In 1950, there were 1.5 million people in Oregon. Twenty years later, there were more than two million. Population was overwhelmingly concentrated in Portland, and suburbia was starting to sprawl into the rich, productive farmlands of the Willamette Valley. Houses, freeways, and shopping centers were replacing fruit orchards, dairies, and hop farms. The Republican governor, Tom McCall, who was famous for his colorful speech, told people on CBS TV, before God and Country, to visit, but not to stay.[121] Naturally, the words had the opposite effect—who wouldn't want to live in a state that was determined to protect itself from uncontrolled growth?

Tom McCall took office on January 9, 1967, replacing Mark Hatfield, who had been elected Senator. With his inaugural address, McCall set out his goals for Oregon. Everything about the state was "tied inseparably to the environment," McCall said. "Water, air, land, and scenic pollution threaten these and other values in Oregon. The overriding challenge of the decade is the issue of quality of life in Oregon."[122]

In July 1967, Tom McCall signed the Beach Bill, which guaranteed public access to the beach along the entire length of the state. The Bottle Bill was passed requiring deposits on beer and soft drink containers to discourage littering. Regulations were passed to clean up the rivers in the state, to establish a greenway along the Willamette River, to require the state's highway trust fund to support bike paths and other amenities for cyclists.[123]

But it was with Senate Bill 100 that Tom McCall's reputation was made. In 1973, McCall referred to "...unfettered despoiling of the land," and "Sagebrush subdivisions, coastal condomania, and the ravenous rampage of suburbia [that] threaten to mock Oregon's status as an environmental model." Oregon, he said, must be protected from "the grasping wastrels of the land."[124]

The original proponent of land use reform in Oregon was a state senator named Hector Macpherson. Owner of a dairy farm in rural Linn County, he saw the fertile soil of the Willamette Valley being buried under asphalt and subdivisions. Not all farmers were unhappy about getting top dollar for a farm that their children didn't want to run; selling out was a retirement package and many were eager to strike a deal. But Macpherson and Tom McCall, and McCall's successor, Robert Straub, saw disaster ahead. They were not "environmentalists" as the term was used later; all of them expected the land use laws to protect timber lands as well as farm lands so that they could support jobs and contribute to the financial health of the state. But if the state didn't take action, and soon, they feared that Oregon's much-vaunted quality of life would disappear.[125]

It wasn't just the populous counties in the Willamette Valley that needed controls over "unlimited and unregulated growth."[126] Jefferson County, on the east side of the Cascades, had a mere 8,506 residents in 1970, but developers were moving in to take advantage of the lack of zoning. The developers wanted to create new subdivisions for which the county had no rational way to provide services. The County Commissioners appealed to the governor for help.

Jefferson County, however, was the exception. Most rural counties had no zoning and didn't want any. Why have zones for industrial, residential, and commercial use in Wheeler County, population 1,849 in 1970? Or gigantic Harney County on the east side of the state? There were so few people scattered across so much Harney County sagebrush that Crane Union High School provided dormitories because it was impractical to gather up students from far-flung ranches every day, some of them more than 150 miles away.

Most coastal counties also lacked zoning. Lincoln County, at the center of the coast, had development zoning along the beaches, which allowed for higher density residential and some tourist commercial development, but the rest of the county was open to just about anything. The most restrictive zone in the county was A-1, which allowed five-acre residential development on agricultural forestland. According to Matt Spangler, former planning director for Lincoln County, when Senate Bill 100 was passed, "It was probably the largest downzoning ever....pretty safe to say it hasn't been replicated anywhere in the United States."[127]

Lane County, the next county south along the coast, had the added complications of the Eugene-Springfield Metro Area, but in the rural areas, minimal to no zoning was fairly typical of all the counties of western Oregon, Spangler explained.

Much of the early effort to control how land was used in Oregon was directed toward preserving farmland. L.B. Day was a state legislator and the first director of the state's Department of Environmental Quality. He was also an official with the Teamsters Union in Marion County, south of Portland, and concerned that loss of farmland would mean loss of jobs in the food-producing industries.[128] As population grew, suburbs around the cities in the Willamette Valley were gobbling up prime agricultural land. Day introduced a bill that proposed financial incentives for farmers willing to commit to keeping their land in exclusive farm use. Although his bill wasn't passed by the 1967 legislative session, it led to legislative hearings that provided additional documentation about the ongoing destruction of productive farmland and the impact of uncontrolled suburban sprawl.

The result of the hearings was a package of four bills, Senate Bills 10-13, all aimed at growth management. Governor McCall supported passage. However, the only one that became law was SB 10, which required every county in the state to "plan and zone all their land by January 1, 1972." The stick was that if they failed to complete the process by the deadline, the state would do it for them. There was no carrot—meaning no funds were appropriated, creating a major challenge, particularly for rural counties, which generally had no experienced land use planners. The bill also lacked specific standards to meet environmental goals, such as preserving air and water quality, protecting natural and scenic resources, and of course conserving prime farmlands.

Limited as it was, SB 10 generated opposition "among rural property owners and elected officials, primarily on the coast and in eastern and southern Oregon."[129] McCall threw his energy and his reputation into fighting a ballot measure titled, "Restricts Governmental Power over Rural Property." In classic style, McCall told the voters that if they were going to pass Ballot Measure 11, they might as well replace him as governor since he "didn't want to preside over the degradation of the state's livability."[130]

The ballot measure was soundly defeated in the November 1970 election, but by the time the 1972 deadline arrived for counties to submit their plans, less than a third had done so. Rural counties were particularly resistant; they also lacked the budgets to support an intensive planning process. Absent statewide standards, the quality of the plans that were developed was uneven.[131]

Finally, Senate Bill 100 was introduced and passed in the 1973 legislative session. It was signed into law by Governor Tom McCall as the Oregon Land Use Planning Act (ORS 197).[132]

One of the major changes negotiated in the Senate required the Land Conservation and Development Commission, which would be established under the new law, to be responsible for developing statewide goals and guidelines. Also, local government compliance with the Goals was mandatory. This corrected a major flaw in the earlier bill, SB 10.

Passage of SB100 was just the beginning of Oregon's efforts to control growth. Now the state had to figure out how to administer the law, which mandated that all counties and cities produce a comprehensive land use plan by 1975. Working out the specifics required intense give-and-take between environmental activists and the pro-growth community. The governor appointed members to the Land Conservation and Development Commission (LCDC).

Committees and subcommittees went to work to figure out what SB 100 required and what could practically be achieved. Many of the compromises affected land use planning on the coast, and some would have a direct effect on the Big Creek controversy. In turn, Big Creek would change the way the law was implemented—by opening up the process to increased citizen input.

~

From the beginning, coastal development issues were a challenge. Governor McCall felt a personal connection to the coast, to keep it free of ugly developments and to preserve public access. By the 1970s, while jobs in timber and fisheries were declining due to natural and man-made resource depletion, development pressures on the coast were increasing. Pro-growth members of county commissions and port commissions were eager to see the kind of economic benefits that would come with development of port facilities on the coast's major estuaries. Wetlands were drained for development and estuaries were filled. Condos and resorts were popping up in response to the increasing numbers of retirees moving here and to tourism promotion. Strip development along the highways marred the beauty of the coast landscape. There was virtually no planning and no coordination among the different coastal communities as each competed for development dollars. Infrastructure was inadequate and in some counties—Lincoln was one of them—sewage flowed across the beaches.[133]

In 1971, the Oregon Coast Conservation and Development Commission was established to study the problems and to recommend solutions. However, the Commission didn't move fast enough to keep up with development pressures. The Commission was hampered by lack of funding as well as a membership that was skewed to development interests. The Commission consisted of twenty-four designated local elected officials from coastal communities who generally had a pro-growth perspective, plus six at-large members appointed by the governor. "It's fair to say that local officials dominated the membership," according to Matt Spangler.[134]

Two environmental organizations, the Oregon Environmental Council and the Oregon Shores Conservation Coalition, were highly critical of both the lack of progress and lack of scientific expertise involved in coastal planning. Environmentalists began to put pressure on the governor to freeze development in critical areas along the coast.

In May 1973, the Oregon Student Public Interest Group published a study that was highly critical of the Oregon Coast Conservation and Development Commission. The report insisted that the Commission had to take a regional approach to planning and base its decisions on science. They claimed that local governments were often "captured" by pro-growth interests and not capable of making "hard decisions about land use that were attentive to environmental harm."[135]

Originally, coastal land and estuaries were designated as Areas of Critical Statewide Concern, for which the Land Conservation and Development Commission would prepare objectives and regulations. Shorelands designations were also part of the original legislation, requiring such wide margins along all waterways in the state where no development could take place that opponents argued it would bring all growth to a crashing halt.[136] This was resisted by local governments, agencies, and development interests as too restrictive and planning by the state rather than local governments; it dropped off the page early. Environmentalists were deeply disappointed, calling the decision "a mistake and a tragedy...."[137]

Coastal development continued to be a critical issue. Environmental groups advocated for areas of statewide significance. The coast would clearly be at the top of that list. They wanted strong controls over any development, including goals and guidelines for such activities. They believed that local governments, under pressure from developers, would not be able to protect coastal resources.

These issues generally had more to do with siting port facilities at the major estuaries along the coast, but if the coast had been declared an area of statewide concern, it might have influenced how coastal counties dealt with development of any type. Resorts like Big Creek, which often included construction of vacation homes, tended to turn into scattered pockets of urbanization, exactly the sort of development in a rural area that SB100 was intended to curtail.

After five years of development and public review, the Oregon Coastal Management Plan was adopted in 1977, and approved by the Federal Office of Coastal Zone Management in the United States Department of Commerce. It was the second coastal management plan approved in the nation. Now Oregon had a blueprint to "balance the great benefits of, and demands for, the valuable and vulnerable land and water resources of the Oregon Coast."[138] Also, four new goals were added to the Statewide Planning Goals: Estuaries; Shorelands; Beaches and Dunes; and the Ocean.

~

The role of citizens in land use planning was controversial. Not only did environmentalists want public involvement in the goal-setting process, but they were also determined to have a strong appeals process to counter what they saw as a tendency for local governments to bow to development interests. The League of Women Voters supported this view, suggesting not only that citizens should be directly involved in setting goals and guidelines, but also that "standing to appeal should be construed broadly to encourage citizen involvement."[139]

Vic Atiyeh, then a Republican state senator from the Portland metro area and later governor of Oregon, wanted a narrow definition that required demonstrable harm before anyone could challenge a land use decision. Atiyeh suggested language requiring a party to be "adversely affected" or "aggrieved" by a provision of an adopted comprehensive plan in order to have standing to appeal.[140]

SB 100 did broaden citizen participation. It provided for extensive citizen participation in the development of the Statewide Planning Goals. Once adopted, the goals themselves (Goal 1, Citizen Involvement) mandated that cities and counties insure "...the opportunity for citizens to be involved in all phases of the planning process" during the development and adoption of comprehensive plans.[141] However, the rules defining who could bring a formal legal challenge to an individual land use decision by a local government—such as the zone change that would eventually be granted by Lane County for the Big Creek Resort proposal—were not as clearly articulated. The limits on eligibility to file an appeal of a local land use decision—"standing" in legal parlance—proved a central stumbling block to the resort opponents in their battle against the Big Creek Resort.

~

Compared to many Oregon counties, Lane County was ahead of the curve after SB100's requirements went into effect. While most rural counties had no zoning at all, Lane County had been zoned since 1947, at least in part because of the energy and expertise available from the University of Oregon and its Bureau of Governmental Research and Service, both located in Eugene, the county seat. The Eugene-Springfield Metro Area was the second largest urban area in the state, with 79,028 people in 1970. Even so, it was still far behind the Portland Metro Area, which was home to more than a

million people at the start of that decade. But Eugene-Springfield, at
the south end of the Willamette Valley, was growing, offering
educational opportunities, high tech jobs, reasonable housing
prices, and a quality of life that became even more appealing after
Governor McCall made his famous statement inviting people to
"visit but don't stay."

Lane County is big—4,620 square miles extending from the
crest of the Cascades on the east to the Coast Range and the Pacific
Ocean on the west. Most of the county was rural in the 1970s; it still
is. Timber was a strong industry, generating jobs and revenue from
privately owned industrial forests and from payments to local
governments for harvests on BLM and National Forest lands, which
was intended to make up for the fact that 48 percent of the county's
land area was owned by the tax-exempt Federal government.

SB100 required all counties and municipalities to prepare
comprehensive plans and make their zoning ordinances consistent
with those plans. Archie Weinstein, one of the three Lane County
Commissioners at the time, was opposed to the state telling
counties what to do. He was so resistant that the county planning
department was instructed not to work on the statewide planning
program. Instead, they developed a comprehensive plan based on
watersheds. They were "doing fantastic planning," according to
Kent Howe, then a young county planner who went on to serve as
the planning director before he retired in 2013. "It just wasn't the
state's program."[142]

Six watershed basins were identified in the county: the Upper
and Lower Willamette, the Upper and Lower McKenzie, the Long
Tom, and the Siuslaw (into which they dumped all the ocean tribs,
such as Big Creek, even though they weren't properly part of the
Siuslaw drainage). Each watershed sub-area was analyzed using a
"natural-resource-based planning approach," as Howe describes it.
It's what resource planners began doing two decades later, with

salmon restoration programs. In the 1970s, it was a very innovative approach.[143]

Unfortunately, this was not what the state had in mind. In spite of their pride in the work they'd done, the planning staff had their knuckles rapped when they sent their plan to the Department of Land Conservation and Development for review. It was sent back and they were told to follow the SB100 guidelines. "There were long eighty-hour weeks revamping the good work we'd done on the sub-area plans," Howe remembers, "and retrofitting it into the comprehensive plan."[144] In 1982, the new Lane County Comprehensive Plan was submitted to the Department for review.

The timing of Lane County's Comprehensive Plan development coincided with Vic Renaghan's plans to build his Big Creek Resort in the far northwest corner of the county, although even if he had tried to build it twenty years earlier, he would still have had to apply for a zone change from Lane County's timber designation zone.

John Gray, who developed two destination resorts in the state, did so when few counties had any strong zoning policies. A Portland businessman, he owned Omark Industries. Its subsidiary was Oregon Saw Chain. Under Gray's leadership, company engineers designed and patented the first really good tooth and guard link design for the chains on modern chainsaws, which proved very profitable.

Gray has been called a visionary for his well-designed developments—Salishan on the coast in Lincoln County, and Sun River in the high desert south of Bend in Deschutes County. Both grew into residential communities, the sort of urbanized development in rural areas that SB 100 was intended to discourage. Gray was a strong supporter of the state's land use regulations, was involved in establishing the state's land use watchdog, 1000 Friends of Oregon, and served on the Oregon Environmental Council, but some environmentalists question whether his two signature resorts ever should have been built.

~

When Lane County's Comprehensive Plan was submitted to DLCD for approval, it included the zone change that would clear the way for Vic Renaghan to build his Big Creek Resort. In the end, it also provided tools to the resort opponents who used the appeals process set up in the Land Use Planning Act to object to the intrusion of development in an undeveloped rural location.

CHAPTER TWELVE
THE BOARD OF COUNTY
COMMISSIONERS

...the disputes of your sort come out of the conflicts between two sacred precepts of the Republic, private property rights and America's natural heritage.

—E.O. Wilson, *Anthill: A Novel,* 2010

Ed Meyrowitz was purple with rage. "Now they've done it!" he shouted. "Those fuckers on the coast just gave it away!"[145]

He had a copy of *The Register-Guard* in his hand open to an article announcing that on August 5, 1981, the Board of County Commissioners had overturned the West Lane Planning Commission's decision on Vic Renaghan's request for a zone change on Big Creek. The zoning was changed to Tourist/Commercial on twenty-six acres in the northwest corner of the property where the resort would be built, and Conservation/Recreation/Prime Wildlife on the rest of the property. None of the opponents of the resort knew about the hearing, although it wasn't because "those guys were asleep,"[146] as Meyrowitz believed. The only announcement that Renaghan's zone change request was to be heard appeared as a small notice in *The Register-Guard,* published on July 11.

The notice was for "a public hearing... in Harris Hall, Lane County Courthouse." The matter to be heard was:

1. Proposed "Renaghan" Amendment to the Coastal Subarea Plan, to redesignate 186 acres of land adjacent to Big Creek from 'Natural Resource: Timber' to a combination of 'Tourist/Commercial' and 'Conservation/Recreation/Open Space.'

2. Proposed exception to LCDC Goal No. 4 (Forest Lands) to permit the above redesignations to be made in the Plan.

3. Proposed rezoning of the above-described Renaghan property from Forest Management (FM) District to a combination of Tourist Commercial and Natural Resource (TC/NR) Districts.

Information was available at the Lane County Planning Division, Public Service Building in Eugene.[147]

~

The notice was mailed to Victor and Linda Renaghan, as well as to the Siuslaw National Forest headquarters in Corvallis, the Oregon State Highway Commission, and to Elizabeth Starker, who were all "record owners of real property within at least 250 feet" of the Renaghans' Big Creek property.[148] The other "interested parties," the people who had testified at the West Lane Planning Commission hearings and who thought the matter had been settled by the unanimous vote on April 8 to deny the zone change, knew nothing about the hearing. None of them had obtained the bulky document, "Findings of Fact." No notices of the hearing were posted on the property and there were no notifications published in the local Florence paper, the *Siuslaw News*.

The Renaghans had submitted their request for a zone change more than a year earlier, before they even had title to the property. The original application for an amendment to the county's comprehensive plan and a zone change was filed on June 8, 1979. At that time, the Board of Commissioners had to determine if the application should be reviewed by the county. That decision was postponed until November 14, 1979, when the Board considered the application as part of the initial screening process for plan amendments. They postponed a decision again because of the planning department's heavy workload—this was when the planning department was scrambling to meet the requirements of SB100 following the rejection of their earlier submittal.

On July 30, 1980, the Board voted to allow the Renaghans to proceed. The planning department staff was directed to schedule a public hearing before the West Lane Planning Commission. On April 8, 1981, after three meetings, the WLPC had unanimously denied both the zone change and the change to the comprehensive plan.

More opportunities--and more effective opportunities—for public involvement in planning would be one of the most significant achievements of SB100, and the County Commissioners' "failure to communicate" would end up as the basis for an appeal to the Land Use Board of Appeals by Friends of the Oregon Coast, the group Tom Smith and other members of the opposition organized to fight the development. That appeal eventually wound its way to the Oregon Supreme Court. But for now, the Big Creek opposition was scrambling to respond effectively to the Commissioners' vote to reverse the West Lane Planning Commission decision.

~

Ed Meyrowitz channeled his fury about the Big Creek decision into a plan to challenge the Board of Commissioners' decision. He and his girlfriend, Cecelia Ostrow, had formed a small organization called Natural Earth Foundation. It was, as Cecelia described it, "to be something like OWC, [the Oregon Wilderness Coalition] not competition exactly, but more spiritual and more radical, based on [Ed's] ideas about the woods."[149]

The spiritual part was vital to both Ed and Cecelia. From the time they met in January 1981, they had developed a close bond based on their intimate connections with nature. Ed took Cecelia to places in the Cascades where he went to feel the strength of the earth, to re-charge spiritually, to seek calm in a life that was often filled with turmoil. He taught her to meditate in a special way that eliminated the separation between what was human and what was natural.

Cecelia was open to this spiritual connection. In her book of essays, *Touching the Earth*, she describes her sense of a door opening, showing her what the world was once like, the "real world," a world where the song of a water ouzel had words that she could understand.[150] Her connection to the natural world met Ed's, and broke down his deep sense of alienation. They worked together on a number of projects, including producing a show on public-access television called *Naturesource*. The first show, filmed with a borrowed hand-held video camera, was about Big Creek. Filmed on location, it showed Tom Smith and Tony Cole talking about their plans to stop the resort, although the quality of both the picture and the sound left a lot to be desired. "Still," Cecelia wrote, "it got the information out."[151]

Big Creek was a special place for both of them. They visited Ed's friends, the brothers Tony and Pip Cole, at their place up Big Creek Road. They camped in the area. It was a place Cecelia would return to even after she and Ed were no longer a couple. Cecelia sat at the foot of her favorite old spruce tree, seeking guidance and gaining an understanding that the real reason people felt it was okay to cut down all of the old growth forest was because they were alienated "from the Earth and from each other."[152]

~

The Oregon Wilderness Coalition was formed in 1974, as Andy Kerr, one of the founders put it, by "four zealots who needed stationery."[153] Its mission was to coordinate efforts to protect the natural environment of Oregon. Timber sales were increasing and what was left of the original forests that once covered the western part of the state from the Cascades to the coast was disappearing. By the early 1980s, less than ten percent of the old-growth trees remained.

Tom Smith joined the Oregon Wilderness Coalition soon after the Big Creek opposition formed. By 1984, he was on the board and in 1986 he was elected president. In some ways, the organization was similar to the National Wildlife Federation, known as "The Fed," where Tom had worked in Washington DC. Like The Fed, it was a non-profit association of individuals and groups with an interest in protecting the environment. In 1981, there were 2,000 individual members and 80 organizations in the Oregon Wilderness Coalition, including sportsmen (fishers and hunters), and conservation, recreation, and education organizations. In responding to the Lane County Commissioners' decision on Big Creek, Oregon Wilderness Coalition executive director James Monteith noted, "thirteen of their member organizations were based in Lane County, and nearly one-quarter of the individual members were Lane County residents."[154]

However, in other ways, the Coalition was very unlike The Fed. Andy Kerr was one of the founders, and "the most famous environmental activist in Oregon"[155] during the state's timber wars, according to Jeff Mapes, formerly a columnist with *The Oregonian* and now with Oregon Public Broadcasting (OPB). Kerr is "no longer the enfant terrible of the Oregon environmental movement," Mapes said in an August 2015 article, but during the 1980s, "his provocative sound bites helped turn clear-cut logging into a national issue, while making him a reviled figure in timber country."[156]

Tom Smith brought a different kind of energy to the environmental cause. As Andy Kerr recalled, Tom had more than "an unswerving passion for the natural world." He also had "organizational skills, an ability to lead and to calm some of the wilder egos, and a sense of how to be most effective in the battles to save the environment."[157] That calm, and a deep knowledge of how things were done, was essential to the survival of the Oregon Wilderness Coalition after the brutal battles of the 1970s and early 80s, when it was an organization at war. Members of the Coalition believed—probably with good reason—that they were in a last-ditch battle to save what could be saved of the forests that once covered Oregon like a deep-pile blanket, where free-flowing rivers provided the best, and in many cases, the only way through the woods. Not only did they take on the timber industry, they fought to save the rivers themselves from a frenzy of dam building that Oregon's popular senator, Mark Hatfield, brought to the state.

Hatfield was a formidable foe. He was a pacifist, the only senator to vote against the Tonkin Gulf resolution that escalated the war in Southeast Asia. He was anti-war, anti-abortion, anti-capital punishment. For the mostly liberal environmental community, that was two out of three, and he had many supporters in the state across party lines. The internal conflicts within the environmental community turned the timber wars into a bloody fight, according to James Monteith. People divorced, families broke up, people died from the stress.[158]

By the time they could claim victory, the leaders of the Oregon Wilderness Coalition were bruised and battered. Where to go from here? It was so bad that James Monteith was ready to leave. During this difficult time, he recalled, Tom Smith stopped by OWC's office whenever he was in Salem. He'd grab Monteith and say, "Let's get a bite. Let's have lunch." His steady presence and wise counsel were like a gift, Monteith said, a gift just for him. "To others, he was an ordinary guy, but to me, he was the older, wiser guy, a gift to me out of the blue. He knew exactly what was needed. I still miss him."

Monteith stayed on until 1991, when shifts in policy and strategy convinced him it was time to leave the organization, which by then was called the Oregon Natural Resource Council. He took a position in Washington DC. The staff gave him a parting gift, a pintail duck carved by Tom. The sculpture is still in his kitchen, and he dusts it carefully every week.[159]

Within a week of the Board of Commissioners' decision on Renaghan's zone change application, a meeting was scheduled at the Oregon Wilderness Coalition's office in Eugene to discuss Big Creek. Tom Smith and Tony Cole drove over from the coast. Bob Warren, already a member of the organization, was also present. Andy Kerr, then the executive director, sat at a desk in the front of the room.

What was needed was pressure to re-open the hearing on Big Creek. Andy suggested that Tom and the other folks on the coast formalize Friends of the Oregon Coast and begin raising money and organizing letter-writing campaigns.[160]

Ed Meyrowitz showed up at the meeting filled with righteous anger. He had plans for fighting the resort development, but he felt marginalized by the Oregon Wilderness Coalition regulars. Cecelia, new to the environmental movement, also found the group hard to deal with, at least at first. She came to have great respect for their efforts to save wilderness areas in Oregon, but at the time, she found the Wilderness Coalition guys intimidating. They were smart and maybe a little arrogant. "If you didn't have your facts straight," she recalled, "or if you didn't look right or if you didn't know the right people, they might not talk to you very kindly."[161]

No one intimidated Ed, though. His passion for Big Creek was deep and personal, but he also saw the fight against the resort as an opportunity to make his Natural Earth Foundation a viable player in the environmental wars. In that, he was completely frustrated. As he saw it, Friends of the Oregon Coast was now Andy Kerr's creation; he had already lost control. Nonetheless, he and Cecelia flung themselves into the efforts to drum up public support for a new hearing.[162]

Letters were sent to the Editor's Mailbox at *The Register-Guard*. Most pointed out the undeveloped nature of the Big Creek site and the negative impact a large commercial development would have on the area. Alexis Petrohilos of Eugene wrote, "There are places that cannot be given a dollar price... It is somewhat ridiculous to assume that we as people with unchallenged destructive power have the right to sell such a cradle of life and guarantee its obliteration."[163]

"It is tragic," Alexis continued, "that a county that holds such rich and beautiful country can take these things for granted and seal the fate of such beautiful places as Big Creek. It is also tragic that people in important offices making important decisions can be so weak, shortsighted and ignorant that they can be seduced by the dollar and willingly allow the massacre of wilderness. Wilderness is something that cannot rightfully be owned, let alone sold by any mere human."[164]

In a more moderate tone, Tom Smith wrote to the Commissioners on September 25, 1981, urging them to "give everyone interested in testifying adequate opportunity to do so." (underlining in original). The "Findings of Fact," he continued, "contains too many misstatements, irrelevancies, distortions, contradictions, and self-serving statements." How could anyone, he asked, consider the document "findings of fact?"[165]

Jerry Rust, the one Commissioner who voted against the zone change, submitted a letter to *The Register-Guard* in early October, in which he stated that the coast residents had relied on the "strong local expression of legislative intent" of the West Lane Planning Commission's unanimous decision not to approve Renaghan's petition. They had assumed, he wrote, that the issue was closed and made a reasonable decision not to attend the Board of Commissioners' meeting on August 5. It would seem more likely that they simply never looked for an announcement of the hearing. Whatever the case, Rust claimed there is a strong moral question involved, and... the Commission needs to open the record.[166]

Whether they thought the resort should be built or not, people on the coast were irritated that their views were discounted by the Board of Commissioners in Eugene. A September 13, 1981 editorial in *The Siuslaw News* defended decisions by the West Lane County Planning Commission as reflecting local conditions. People had fought to have this branch of the County Planning Commission located on the coast, and they wanted its decisions respected.[167]

~

Harold Rutherford, the chair of the Lane County Board of Commissioners, represented coastal Lane County. He was a conservative who believed "Government must keep off people's backs and let our free enterprise system work." Although the Board of Commissioners no longer reflected the opposition to SB100 that was expressed by former Commissioner Archie Weinstein, Rutherford believed that "the state's Land Use Program must be made to work for the people, not against them."[168] Decentralizing land use decisions by having a satellite Planning Commission on the coast, while perhaps working for those people who lived on the coast, meant important decisions had a tendency to get away from the direction Chairman Rutherford believed should be followed. Improvement of the county's economy ranked much higher with him than whatever values were reflected in the West Lane Planning Commission's decision to deny Vic Renaghan's zone change request. He also believed that Jerry Rust was "orchestrating the opposition." Rutherford was firmly opposed to reopening the hearing. The resort was "just what the coastal economy needs and having someone like Renaghan on the site will result in better protection of its natural values than just leaving it undeveloped for unlimited public access."[169]

Before deciding to overturn the West Lane Planning Commission decision, the Board of Commissioners had the opportunity to review "all of the materials, information, and documents submitted previously to the West Lane Planning Commission." That information was contained in a lengthy document, Findings of Fact and Conclusions of Law Supporting Approval of Plan Amendment and Zone Change, as well as Conditions of Approval, known as Exhibit B.[170]

The Findings of Fact document closely follows the Coastal Subarea Plan, the Statewide Goals, and various legal precedents. Generally speaking, the planning goals are prescriptive, not proscriptive. In other words, they allow certain activities providing allowance is made for values such as wildlife habitat, scenery, recreational access, or economic development. This perspective seems to lead inexorably toward the conclusion that construction of resort facilities at Big Creek is not prohibited, and that in fact, the resort would support various objectives in the Subarea Plan including tourist facilities, private investment, and economic development.[171]

Statewide Goal 17, Coastal Shorelands, doesn't prohibit development. It simply says that any development has to be based on an analysis of the area, and how development can meet the Coastal Shorelands Goal. Applying the Prime Wildlife Management designation to the Big Creek area meant that proposals by public agencies would need to assess the impact of their actions on wildlife populations. Likewise, Goal 4, Forest Land, didn't require that the Big Creek property be preserved exclusively for timber harvest, only that the Findings had to justify an Exception.

The Oregon Wilderness Coalition focused on the Oregon Silverspot Butterfly as the most important argument against developing the Big Creek property. The habitat on the west side of the highway was the focus of protection policies, but the butterfly, as pointed out in the West Lane Planning Commission hearing, didn't confine itself to the salt spray meadows. Once hatched, the Silverspots moved around, seeking shelter and mates in the forest on the east side of the highway where the resort would be located.

According to the Findings of Fact, however, application of the Prime Wildlife Management designation to the Big Creek property wasn't intended to preserve habitat. Its purpose was analysis and evaluation.[172]

That evaluation was conducted by David McCorkle, a biology professor from Western Oregon State College (now Western Oregon University). Even though he had played a significant role in getting the Silverspot listed under the Endangered Species Act, he had testified before the West Lane Planning Commission that the resort would have no impact on the salt spray meadows west of the highway. He expressed some concern that the insects could be harmed if the resort managers sprayed for mosquitoes around the lodge property, although the Oregon Coast, which is cool and often windy in the summer, is not known as a major breeding ground for mosquitoes. He concluded that the resort "could be a 'boon' to the protection and enhancement of the habitat if certain conditions were met."[173] Under the Conditions of Approval, Vic Renaghan agreed to meet those requirements.

Dr. McCorkle's conclusion differs from that of Dr. Robert M. Pyle, chair of the International Union for Conservation of Nature Lepidoptera Group, of which he was a founder and, at the time of the Big Creek controversy, past president. He was also a board member of the Xerces Society, which works to protect invertebrates and their habitat. His letter to the West Lane Planning Commission during their consideration of Renaghan's zone change request pointed out the perilous condition of *Speyeria zerene hippolyta*, the Oregon Silverspot Butterfly. He was "worried about the potential impact of residents of the new development on the [salt spray] meadows" and the adjacent woodlands. The plight of the Silverspot is a matter of concern to people involved in organizations for science and conservation all over the world, he noted. Recognizing that it is a challenge to balance the conflicting benefits of economic development and habitat protection, Dr. Pyle concluded, "Our joint feeling is that the resource represented by the indicator species, the Silverspot, and its utterly unique habitat, is an irreplaceable feature of Lane County and of the Maritime Northwest: a resource which should be safeguarded."[174]

The Oregon Wilderness Coalition pointed out that Dr. McCorkle, who was retained by the Renaghans, was not hired to "determine the best actions on behalf of the endangered butterfly." His role was to "suggest possible methods of mitigation." He seemed reluctant to antagonize the developer, since he hoped that a cooperative relationship would best serve the Silverspot population. The Oregon Wilderness Coalition insisted, "The best course of action for the federally listed Oregon Coastal Silverspot Butterfly is no action."[175] This option was not considered in the staff report.

When Renaghan bought the Big Creek property, the zoning allowed him to harvest timber. Statewide Goal #4 made retention of timberlands a high priority; counties needed to justify actions that would remove lands from timber production. In the Findings of Fact, considerable discussion focused on the management of surrounding properties by the Forest Service and State Parks. Since these agencies "managed and maintained almost exclusively for scenic quality, recreational use, wildlife habitat, and roadless areas," and since the Highway 101 corridor on this part of the coast "is an area of high visual sensitivity," timber production at Big Creek was considered undesirable.[176]

There was no argument from the opponents of the resort on this count. The real difference of opinion was over how the property should be used since timber harvest was undesirable. The discussion shifted seamlessly to tourism since the scenic and habitat values of the surrounding properties were being preserved to enhance tourist and recreational experiences, rather than as habitat for wildlife. When discussing who—or what—gets to use the land, the discussion is nearly always human-centric. This is not subtle— the Coastal Subarea's Planning for People contains the goal of preparing "for future growth, particularly recreation and tourism."

The Findings of Fact pointed out that tourism was increasing in Oregon generally, and on the coast in particular. In Lane County, as employment in timber and wood products declined during the 1970s, tourism-related employment increased. The decrease in the former (17.5 percent) was almost equal to the increase in the latter (15.8 percent), although of course, different demographic sectors were affected. And although campgrounds, day use areas, and hiking trails dot this portion of the coast, there were no facilities of the type proposed by Renaghan—restaurants, stores, or lodging at a resort facility.

Highway 101 between Florence and Yachats has a lot of scenery, but no private accommodations other than a few cabins and small motels. No public monies were available to remedy this shortage. The report claimed that this made the need for private investment even stronger.[177]

In conclusion, the Findings of Fact states that the plan amendment proposed by Renaghan didn't "conflict with any specific textual provision, goal, or policy statement contained in the Subarea Plan," particularly as related to the commitment to increasing tourism and decreasing timber production.[178]

The irony of the Findings is that it relies on the very qualities that the resort opponents wanted to protect to justify making the zone changes that would allow the resort to be developed. The Oregon Wilderness Coalition submitted a letter to the Commissioners on September 28, pointing out the flaws in the Silverspot evaluation and the failure to respond to concerns expressed by the Oregon Department of Fish & Wildlife about overfishing the creek. The Findings dismissed those concerns, noting that the resort would not be built next to the creek, just as it dismissed concerns about elk habitat, claiming that the resort wouldn't interfere with elk habitat. While the Findings used the adjacent roadless area at Rock Creek, which was then under consideration as a Wilderness Area, to justify the need for more tourist accommodations, the Oregon Wilderness Coalition clearly saw a destination resort that close to the Wilderness Area as a negative. They requested that the Commission "conduct public hearings in Florence and Eugene to take testimony on these flaws and errors."[179]

~

The final decision on the zone change and plan amendment was on the Board of Commissioner's agenda for October 6, 1981. The opponents increased the pressure. Friends of the Oregon Coast organized a rally at the courthouse on the Friday of Labor Day weekend. About sixty people attended; nearly everyone was opposed to the Big Creek Resort.

According to Cecelia Ostrow, she and Ed "ate and breathed and slept Big Creek."[180] Because they were in Eugene, Ed made himself useful, filing the incorporation papers for Friends of the Oregon Coast, and picking up and banking donations. Donations generally came through the Oregon Wilderness Coalition since it was a tax-exempt organization and donors could deduct contributions from their federal taxes. It was one of the functions they performed for the environmental organizations in the coalition.

In a frenzy, Ed popped out one idea after another. He tried to organize a land swap with the U.S. Forest Service. He contacted other environmental groups to see if anyone would buy the Big Creek property as a nature preserve. He tried to get National Geographic to do a special on Big Creek. He and Cecelia showed their video of Tom Smith and Tony Cole at Big Creek on their public-access TV program, *Naturesource.* They followed the Big Creek elk herd up onto the ridge, dragging camera equipment, to document, as Cecelia said, "what was being displaced by the resort."[181]

Ed and the Natural Earth Foundation, Andy Kerr on behalf of the Oregon Wilderness Coalition, and Barbara Wright of Greenpeace started a petition drive to order a referendum on the adoption of County Commissioners' Ordinance 852, which would change the zone and the comprehensive plan designation for Big Creek. They requested that the County Commissioners re-open the public hearing. By the beginning of October, they had 700 signatures, and expected the list to reach 1,000 by the time of the hearing on October 6.

But tensions began to develop between Ed and the people on the coast. His one-man-show style was bound to rankle. Friends of the Oregon Coast was a coalition of volunteers. No one was getting paid. Bob Warren recalled that Ed "got in the way."[182] There were some questions about Ed's accounting of the money that had been donated to the Big Creek campaign. When the Friends held a meeting in Florence, the two hundred people who attended applauded Ed's speech, but they turned to Tony and Tom—people known in the local community—for answers to their questions.[183] Tom was elected president, Tony Cole was the vice-president, Bob

Warren was the secretary, and Owen Harrington was the treasurer. Ed's pyrotechnic style was completely out of sync.

Eventually the Friends handed Ed a letter. They thanked him for all he had done for Big Creek, but there was no room in the organization for someone who couldn't work with the group. They accused him of "ignoring group advice and acting without group consent." He was asked to resign and to produce complete financial records.[184]

~

On October 1, County Counsel William Van Vactor presented a memorandum to the Board of Commissioners regarding their options in responding to the "substantial amount of written material" objecting to the Findings of Fact and Conclusions of Law. Van Vactor noted that none of the letter writers had appeared before the Board at the hearing on August 5, nor had any of them attended the West Lane Planning Commission hearings.[185]

An additional twenty-two letters were filed objecting to the application in general, plus a photo of Big Creek submitted by Ed Meyrowitz, and thirty-three pages of signed petitions protesting the zone change. All the material was received after the public hearing was closed, Van Vactor pointed out, and the Commissioners were not legally obligated to re-open the hearing. Should they choose to do so, Van Vactor said, Renaghan had to be given the right to respond. This would mean sending out new notices and setting a time and place for another hearing.[186]

Van Vactor prepared two motions for the Commissioners to consider. The first was a motion to adopt Order 852 and approve the Renaghan application for plan amendment and the intent to rezone, and to adopt the Findings of Fact. The second was a motion to re-open the hearing, in which case, Van Vactor advised, the Commissioners should defer consideration of the Findings.

The Board went with the first option, voting 4 to 1 to adopt Order 852, with conditions for approval (Exhibit B) that had to be met before the zone change was final.

The resort opponents now turned to the Land Use Board of Appeals.

CHAPTER THIRTEEN
THE LAND USE BOARD OF APPEALS

The town of Yachats wasn't much more than a wide spot in the road in the 1970s when Jim and Ursula Adler arrived in his vintage Jeep, searching for an artists' community, a place to live where he could set up his forge. They met the local potter in his shop, were invited home for a lunch of fresh-caught Dungeness crab, and ended up buying ten acres on the Yachats River Road, about three miles east of the town. They began building a house and a shop.

They met Tom and Billie Jo Smith at a dinner hosted by the Reverend Robert Hoggard and his girlfriend, Starr. Hoggard had been Canon Pastor at Grace Cathedral in San Francisco under Bishop James Pike. He left that position and moved to Yachats, where he bought the local gas station, hired someone to man the pumps, and settled back to enjoy coastal life. Starr was eager to meet a more sophisticated social circle, so she looked around and found a few couples who at least had a college education. She invited them to dinner—the Adlers, the Smiths, and a third couple, the Reims—and served caviar on baked potatoes. She told everyone what a delicacy it was.

"It was Sacramento River caviar," Jim recalled. "It was terrible."[187] He looked across the table and met Billie Jo's eye, which was twinkling with amusement. The Adlers and the Smiths became close friends. After Jim landed the contract to forge fireplace tools for Norm Thompson, Tom often came up to the shop and helped them with production, packaging, and shipping.

Tom and Jim bonded instantly, but Jim didn't get too involved in the Big Creek issue until after the Board of Commissioners' decision on the zone and comprehensive plan changes. By that time, Jim had been appointed to the Planning Commission of Lincoln County.

"I was learning a lot about Senate Bill 100 and the state planning goals, and I thought I had something to contribute" to the fight against the resort development at Big Creek, Jim remembered.[188]

~

With approval of SB 100 and the requirement that all counties and cities in Oregon prepare comprehensive land use and zoning plans, it was inevitable that there would be conflicts over both policy and specific zoning decisions as they affected people's property. At first, appeals were heard by the Land Conservation and Development Commission and the circuit courts. The Land Use Board of Appeals, usually referred to as LUBA, was created in 1979. It's a separate quasi-judicial, three-person appeals board. The board members, called referees, are appointed by the governor, and have to be members of the Oregon State Bar. They serve four-year terms. When the Big Creek appeal reached LUBA, at the end of 1981, Michael D. Reynolds was the Chief Referee; William C. Cox and John T. Bagg were the other members of the Board.

Friends of the Oregon Coast decided to appeal the Lane County Board of Commissioners' decision on Big Creek to the Land Use Board of Appeals. Jim Adler offered to help Tom find a land use attorney in Eugene.

There were not a lot of choices. One, Michael Farthing, was already working for Vic Renaghan. They made an appointment with Timothy Sercombe and drove to Eugene to talk to him.

Tim Sercombe had started working with the firm of Johnson, Harrang, & Swanson only a few years before. The City of Eugene was one of their clients, so they had done some land use work, but as Tim Sercombe said later, representing a handful of radical environmentalists on the coast—who, it went without saying, wouldn't be able to pay much—was not a very attractive prospect. Nonetheless, he agreed to take on their appeal.[189]

~

LUBA Case No. 81-102 included petitioners Robert Warren, Tony Cole, Ginger Cole, Ed Meyrowitz, and Donna Shelton, one of the West Lane Planning Commissioners. The Renaghans and Lane County were the respondents.

Before any decision could be made on the substantive issues— the reversal of the West Lane Planning Commission denial, the exception to Goal 4, and changing the comprehensive plan—LUBA had to agree that the petitioners had standing, that they were eligible to file the appeal.

Eventually, the Big Creek appeal would change what was required to establish standing, but when the case was filed, petitioners needed to show they were not just aggrieved by a decision, but actually would experience some injury to their personal interests. Tim Sercombe filed affidavits from Tony and Ginger Cole in which they claimed such injury. Construction of the resort would cause significant delays in their use of Big Creek Road, the only route from their house to Highway 101, where their mailbox was located, and which they had to use for any travel to take care of business, shop, or work.[190] The Renaghans and the County said that the claims of damage were not true. After an evidentiary hearing on May 4, 1982, LUBA asked the appellants to provide more support for their claims. Residents on Big Creek Road already experienced delays due to fallen trees and road maintenance. Would the resort really make things that much more difficult? How did it create an adverse condition for the Coles?[191]

Sercombe admitted he wasn't really sure what "adverse" meant in this situation, but he gamely came up with a number of factors that could make it critical for Tony to avoid delays when driving on Big Creek Road. For example, did he need to be at work promptly, perhaps because he was a probationary employee who would lose his job if he arrived late? Or was he likely to experience medical emergencies, where delays could be a matter of life or death? Or, now that Ginger and their three children were living in Florence, did he have a limited amount of time to visit the children such that any delays would cut into his time with them or jeopardize agreements to have them back at their mother's home at a specific time? Sercombe needed Tony to come to his office in Eugene to sign an affidavit. This supporting material was due in a week. He alerted Tony that he might have to appear in person before LUBA. "The success of this appeal stands and falls on this last hurdle," he told Tony.[192]

~

Weeds push up through cracks in the sidewalk in front of Tong King Chinese restaurant in Salem, Oregon, and the asphalt parking lot in back has crumpled and buckled so badly that the white lines of the parking spaces fold in on themselves, leaving the spaces too small for most cars. Inside, the one-story building is divided into three rooms. Small tables are covered with white lace tablecloths protected by glass. The walls are decorated with prints of misty mountains and arched bridges.

It doesn't look at all like the sort of place where judges would go for lunch, but for more than twenty years, Tim Sercombe has been eating lunch here, joining a number of other judges and law clerks on the state bench, including Paul Lindy, a retired State Supreme Court justice who had been a mentor to many of them.

Tim Sercombe was appointed to the state Court of Appeals by Governor Ted Kulongoski in 2007, winning election to the position in 2008, and again in 2014 following an unsuccessful bid for the State Supreme Court. As an appellate judge, he quickly became the go-to guy for land use issues due to his years of experience as an attorney representing developers and city or county governments in land use cases. When Sercombe arrived at Tong King for an interview about the long-term impact of the Friends of the Oregon Coast's LUBA appeal, he was well prepared. (Judge Sercombe retired from the Appellate Court in 2017.)

~

The late 1970s and early 80s, Sercombe explained, was a "great period of contesting whether plans were consistent" with the state's land use planning goals. These were policy issues rather than adjudicative issues because there weren't a lot of comprehensive plans completed and approved yet. Big Creek was one of the first cases in opposition to rural development to go through the courts. "It is perhaps not surprising," he said, "that it went through the court system on sort of a procedural issue."[193]

After the local government sends out the notice of a decision, the appellant has twenty-one days to file and establish standing. The basis for standing had been a controversial topic during the drafting of the SB100 rules.

If appellants were entitled to notice of the decision by the local government, they had standing. Those notices were given to people who were parties to the decision. In the Renaghan case, "parties" was narrowly defined. Notices were sent to the Renaghans and their legal representative, and the owners of properties adjacent to their Big Creek property, which were the Forest Service and Elizabeth Bond Starker. Although Tony and Ginger Cole owned the nearest residence, their property did not have a common boundary with the Renaghans' property, so they did not receive notice.

Another way to establish standing is to claim that the petitioner was harmed or aggrieved. Sercombe explained that this standard is often seen in federal statutes, which use the term *adversely affected*, to determine standing in an appeal for further review of an administrative decision.[194]

The issue of standing and of who is adversely affected by a government decision was being expanded in other arenas as the citizen involvement movement took hold. When decisions were being made about building nuclear power plants in the Pacific Northwest, Lloyd Marbett, an environmental activist in Oregon who was particularly concerned about nuclear power, challenged the decision of the Energy Facility Council to build the Trojan nuclear plant outside Portland. He had first to establish that he had standing, to show that he, and implicitly many others, was adversely affected by having a nuclear power plant in his backyard.

This view was very much in line with SB100's Statewide Planning Goals. Goal #1 is "To develop a citizen involvement program that insures the opportunity for citizens to be involved in all phases of the planning process." The intent was inclusion, not exclusion, starting with establishment of the Statewide Goals and continuing through development of local comprehensive plans and actions that derived from those plans. The League of Women Voters and various environmental groups favored a broad definition. State Senator Victor Atiyeh, who later became governor, argued for a narrow definition. His view prevailed.[195]

Other court cases that preceded the Big Creek appeal also refined the definition of how standing was established, broadening the sense of *adversely affected* and *aggrieved*. Tim Sercombe believes that when the Big Creek case came up, few substantive issues had come before the Land Use Board of Appeals.[196] Even though control over what Governor McCall, not mincing words, called the "scatteration of unimaginative, mislocated urban development introducing little cancerous cells of unmentionable ugliness into our rural landscape"[197] was certainly part of the intent of the framers of SB100, such control was a very new concept in Oregon and everywhere else.

Three years into LUBA's existence, the referees were still working out their procedural rules. Sercombe couldn't recall any cases at the time he filed the Big Creek petition where LUBA had held an evidentiary hearing to determine if there had been a procedural violation.

There was uncertainty about what kind of case this was. A different level of notification was required, depending on whether the Commissioners were considering a policy issue, such as how to define and determine how areas should be treated in drafting the comprehensive plan, or if this was an adjudicative issue, in regard to a specific property or activity. The Renaghans' situation involved a zone change for a very large property and an amendment to the County's Comprehensive Plan. The plan had not yet been finalized by the Land Conservation and Development Commission when the Board of Commissioners approved that amendment. Was it quasi-judicial or quasi-legislative?

"There was always a bit of uncertainty about what was required here," Sercombe said. He argued that the Commissioners should have given individual notice to Tony Cole and the other petitioners in the case because they were participants in the proceeding by virtue of their attendance at the earlier hearing before the West Lane Planning Commission. He believed the law entitled them to receive a notice when that decision was appealed to allow them to continue to participate.[198]

LUBA heard the more detailed arguments about how Tony Cole's travel on Big Creek Road would be delayed, and concluded that his inconvenience was "insufficiently substantial" to give him standing under the statute. LUBA dismissed the case.[199]

It was a frustrating decision, particularly because Chief Referee Michael Reynolds said in his discussion that it was clear that the County made substantive errors when it reversed the West Lane Planning Commission's denial of Renaghan's petition. Sercombe said he didn't know why Reynolds made this comment, but it supported the rest of Sercombe's argument—that the petitioners had standing because they were adversely affected in the sense of aggrieved. They were aggrieved as representatives within the planning area that was affected by this decision, and aggrieved as people who had participated in the previous hearing held by the West Lane Planning Commission. If LUBA had granted standing to Tony Cole, Bob Warren, and the other petitioners, this sense of being aggrieved by a government decision would have flung open the door to increased citizen participation.[200]

~

Friends of the Oregon Coast usually held their meetings at the Waterfront Coffee Company in Old Town Florence, where they could watch fishing boats pass under another of Conde McCullough's handsome bridges.

On January 22, 1982, while the LUBA decision was still pending, FOC members met to discuss how to raise money to cover Tim Sercombe's legal fees. If LUBA declined to hear their case, there would likely be an appeal to the State Court of Appeals. Their attorney may not have had great expectations about their ability to pay, but they felt they needed to make a serious effort to raise money. Fundraisers were also a good way to publicize their cause, educate the public, and gain supporters.

The favored tactic was spaghetti feeds. Dick Schwartz and Kate Kelly, who lived in Yachats, owned a restaurant on the Bayfront in Newport called The Whale's Tale. On days when the restaurant was closed, Kate went in and cooked up gallons of tomato sauce. Tom Smith, Jim and Ursula Adler, Marie Cole and her sister Sarah Scholfield, Stacy Smith, Mila Niemi (who lived in Sarah's cabin when Sarah was traveling), and many others in the "greater Tenmile community" showed up to boil the spaghetti, wait tables, and clean up. Spaghetti dinners were held at the Florence Booster Senior Center, at the Yachats Commons, and at The Whale's Tale itself. Ken Kesey, who owned a house just south of the Tenmile bridge, surprised everyone by showing up unannounced to support the cause. There were events in Eugene also, including a slide show and music at Kona Café near the University of Oregon campus. That event featured a raffle for a weekend on the coast at Jacqueline's See-Vue Motel, a charming collection of uniquely decorated rooms above the beach, with Sunday brunch included. FOC members debated whether to charge $1 or $2 for the raffle tickets. Tom said, "Such a nice prize deserves a larger ticket price." They went with the lower price, hoping to make it up in volume.[201]

They held spaghetti feeds everywhere and all the time. Gallons of sauce, and yards and yards of noodles. Tom put out the word for desserts and baked goods. It was a good time, a natural extension of the dinners and potlucks that fueled the Tenmile community. They generated goodwill, spread the word, made a little money. Tom and Billie Jo were the only people in the community with any money at all, mostly because Billie Jo was the only person with a steady full-time job. Most people had time and energy, and they donated their artwork to auction off to raise money for Big Creek. Ursula and Marie wove colorful shawls. Jim made whimsical candleholders at his forge. Tom carved wooden ducks and made jewelry from stones, shells, and bits of driftwood he found on the beach. They sent whatever they collected to Tim Sercombe—a hundred dollars one month, five hundred the next, nothing at all more often than not.

Besides spaghetti feeds, auctions, and concerts, FOC members sold sausages. The sausages were made by Dennis Rock, who lived up Tenmile Creek Road. FOC members would go anywhere to sell sausages. If there were twelve people gathering for an event, Tom would pull a box of Dennis Rock's sausages out of the freezer, pack up some buns and condiments, arm-twist a few volunteers, and head out to raise money for Big Creek.

The city of Florence holds an event called Rhody Days on Memorial Day weekend to celebrate the wild rhododendrons that bloom amid the shore pine forests near the coast. There's a parade— local high school bands, the Shriners on their funny go-carts, the Sheriff's posse on horseback. Food and craft booths line the highway on the north side of town, as well as in the Old Town district along the river. Friends of the Oregon Coast could set up in either place, Tom was told. There was a space in the Old Town area in front of a bar where, it was rumored, the Free Souls motorcycle gang would hang out.

"Motorcycle guys and Polish sausages? Seems like a no-brainer," Tom said. "Yeah, we'll take that spot." After an hour of standing behind the motorcycles trying to sell sausages, it was obvious that passersby were passing by, generally crossing to the other side of the street to avoid the rowdy-looking guys standing by their big Harleys. The bikers weren't buying either. Hard to be cool with yellow mustard and sauerkraut dripping on your leathers.[202]

~

They weren't any more successful at the Summer Festival in Toledo, a mill town seven miles east of Newport. Back then, the festival was still a small-town event with a couple hundred mostly local folks attending.

Tom, Billie Jo and their friends, Jim and Ursula, had the routine down. The men set up the booth and a camp stove. Billie Jo and Ursula heated a big pot of water and dropped in the fat, pale sausages. Dennis Rock's sausages were filled with garlic and sage. The pungent fragrance should have brought a crowd of people to the booth, but the families wandering around Toledo's Waterfront Park walked right past.

Tom couldn't even give the sausages away. When a boy in an oversized orange Oregon State jersey followed his nose to find out what was cooking, Tom leaned over and offered him a bun with a juicy sausage. "On the house," Tom said. The kid looked dubious. "Free, son. For you."

The boy looked over his shoulder at an invisible line of authority from someone in the crowd. He wrinkled his face ruefully. "Uh, no, that's OK... I mean, thanks, but...." He turned away to re-join his family.

The sausage smell merged with the smell of emissions from the Georgia-Pacific mill and its settling ponds. The Toledo plant manufactures containerboard, the brown paper used to make packaging. The plant has made dramatic progress in dealing with the odors, but back in the early 1980s, you might still notice the smell, depending on which way the wind was blowing or where you were standing in relation to the mill.

Toledo has been a timber town since the early 1900s. In the 1950s, Georgia-Pacific bought the failing C.D. Johnson Lumber Corporation. In the 1980s, the mill employed more than 400 people, although the number has decreased to around 370 as some non-containerboard operations were eliminated. Three shifts operated around the clock, providing family wage jobs in the community—in the mill, in the woods, and for the shops and businesses along Main Street. If there was an odor, it was not a problem. If steam poured out of the mill stacks, it was not a problem. Those jobs paid the rent, paid for a new pickup truck and a couple of hunting rifles, paid for new shoes for the kids, food on the table. If there was a smell, most people just ignored it.

Friends of the Oregon Coast's issue—trying to block a resort located a good hour's drive to the south—was a matter of supreme indifference to the good folks of Toledo on that summer day. They didn't know anything about the plan to build a resort. The property wasn't even in the same county. Most likely, if they had an opinion, it was let them build the damn resort. Who cares? At least it would provide some jobs, always an appealing prospect in the marginal economies of coastal towns.

Still, the folks in Toledo weren't hostile. The northwest timber wars, which would pit loggers against conservationists, were still several years in the future. The Northern Spotted Owl wouldn't be listed as a threatened species under the federal Endangered Species Act for another ten years, although opposition to the intense clear-cutting of the past two decades had started to rally. The owl had been adopted as a symbol of everything that was wrong with timber harvest policies on the national forests. Nonetheless, it was still possible for loggers and newcomers to hang out together, drink a few brews at the local pub, tell tall tales. In the rural valleys of the Coast Range, people lived close to the land, whether they were logging families or new-age homesteaders. The old-timers showed the young urban refugees how to cut firewood, how to set up a water system.

Hippies found work planting trees on the clear-cut slopes, alongside the descendants of early settlers. Some counterculture tree planters organized as Hoedads, forming a co-op to demand better pay and more control over their labor, naming themselves for the mattock-like tool they used to dig holes for the seedling trees. Lane County Commissioner Jerry Rust, the only Commissioner to vote against Renaghan's zone change, was one of the original organizers of the co-op, which Robert Leo Heilman describes in an essay, "With a Human Face: When Hoedads Walked the Earth."[203]

The women from both communities spun their own wool, wove on looms set up in their living rooms, mingled at the county fair. They shared information about raising food, canning, and baking bread.

They weren't hostile, these timber families, but... they were wary. The people in the Friends booth looked like tree-huggers, longhairs, dope-smoking hippies, though Tom didn't quite fit the image. He was too old to be one of them hippie types. Broad-shouldered, barrel-chested, with an unruly gray beard, his long hair held off his face with a bandana, Tom was friendly and outgoing. He leaned across the booth, talking passionately with anyone willing to stop and listen.

"We're raising money to pay a lawyer," he explained to a man who stepped up to the booth. "We want to keep Big Creek natural, a natural area open to everyone." The developer, he said, wants to build a fancy resort on one of the few stretches of the coast between Florence and Yachats that isn't cluttered with tacky motels, gas stations, campgrounds, or vacation cabins. "We're challenging the County Commissioners' decision to approve a zone change that will let this developer build his resort."

"Where is this resort? You talking about the Lincoln County Commissioners?"

"No, no. The development is in Lane County, a couple miles south of Yachats. The Commissioners are in Eugene. The developer's proposal was denied," Tom says, "but the developer appealed and the Commissioners, the Lane County Commissioners, overturned that decision, and—"

"Oh, well," the man cut him off. "Lane County. Bunch-a-hippies over there in Eugene. All those college kids...." The man shrugged. He didn't like Tom's comment about campgrounds. He likes to camp. "I take the family camping every summer. It's a vacation we can afford." He doesn't care about this resort. "You have a good day," he says. "Maybe we'll see you at the games." And he moved on.

Across from the Friends booth, the Toledo Boosters were doing a brisk business selling t-shirts to raise money for the high school teams. The cheerleaders did a pretty routine, their legs flashing under short blue and gold skirts. A kid, maybe a football player, all muscles under his t-shirt, strolled over to the sausage booth.

"Whatcha got in those sausages?" he asked loudly. "Owl meat? Haw haw haw!" He puffed his way back to the appreciative giggling cheerleaders.

Late afternoon sun glared off the Yaquina River. The other Friends members were ready to call it a day. "Let's pack it in," Jim Adler said. A stalwart supporter of Friends of the Oregon Coast and a committed opponent of the resort, Jim could see they weren't going to sell sausages here. People were heading for Memorial Field to watch loggers demonstrate their skills: speed-cutting big logs, climbing poles, chainsaw carving.

With a determined look, Tom grabbed the booth sign and some rope. He wound the rope around the sign and slung it around his neck, suspending the sign to form a tray. Loading up with sausages and buns, he clambered up the stairs into the stands, into the crowd of indifferent loggers and pulp mill workers and their families.

"Get yer sausage! Hot Polish sausage! Get yer sausage. Yes, ma'am, two? Coming up. How about one for you, young lady?" Soon sausages and buns wrapped in waxed paper were traveling hand to hand down the rows, eager fingers reaching for sausages, dollar bills making their way in the opposite direction, back to Tom, who stuffed them inside his shirt. No one asked what he was raising money for, no one sneered "tree hugger." This was about irresistible steaming-hot sausages.

Tom had been the communications director for the National Wildlife Federation. He'd worked in Washington, DC, wore a tie every day, and now he looked like a sandwich board with legs. There could be no doubt: Tom Smith was a dedicated environmentalist.[204]

~

The next step was to take the LUBA decision to the state Court of Appeals, where cases are decided by a panel of three appellate judges. Tim Sercombe argued on behalf of Warren et al, on February 2, 1983.

Lane County was represented by William A. Van Vactor, County Counsel. The Renaghans also entered the case, represented by Portland attorney Stephen T. Janik and Michael Farthing, the Eugene land use attorney who had been representing the Renaghans in the zone change application.

Sercombe was surprised that the Renaghans were still on the case. With LUBA's denial of the standing issue, the Renaghans could have just gone ahead with their plans to build their resort. Instead, the plans were now tied up in legal proceedings.

On April 27, 1983, the three appellate judges, P.J. Richardson, George Van Hoomissen, and J.J. Newman, affirmed the LUBA decision that the delays that Tony Cole might experience on Big Creek Road during construction of the resort were not substantial enough to be considered adverse, and that there was no aggrievement just because the Coles lived in the same general area.[205]

The appellants now turned to the State Supreme Court.

In those days, before you could request a review of an Appellate Court opinion, all ten of the judges of the Court of Appeals had to review the case. They upheld LUBA's denial of standing—but there was dissent. Four of the judges disagreed.

Because of the dissent, the appellants could request a review by the State Supreme Court. The Court agreed to review the case. Again, Tim Sercombe represented the Big Creek opponents.[206]

The State Supreme Court didn't get into adverse effects, and they didn't say the petitioners were aggrieved because of procedure—the failure to receive notice. The appellants, the Court ruled, had standing simply by virtue of the fact that they had participated in the proceeding and were unhappy with the outcome. That made them an aggrieved party with the right to obtain review before the Land Use Board of Appeals.[207]

One effect of Warren v Lane County was to make the legislature clarify what they meant by "standing." Now, if you participate in the local government hearing, you have standing to appeal. It's assumed that if you're filing an appeal, you must be aggrieved by the decision. Participation means an active role—you have to raise the issue at the local hearing, the so-called "raise it or waive it" rule.

"There's no adverse effect thing," Tim Sercombe said. You have to participate in order to have standing, although if you would have been entitled to a notice of a hearing but the local government makes the decision without notifying you, you still have standing to appeal that decision.[208]

Eventually, the Legislature adopted "really detailed statutory requirements for what should happen at the local government hearing," Sercombe explained. The intent was to increase public participation, with the tradeoff that LUBA would have to decide those cases quickly to avoid costly delays to development plans. "In my court," he continued, "which is the Court of Appeals, land use cases are the only cases that we have to get expedited."[209]

The Big Creek decision, and possibly another case Tim Sercombe was involved in regarding plans for a resort on the McKenzie River, stimulated the Department of Land Conservation and Development to propose an amendment to Goal 8, which had to do with recreational needs and the siting of destination resorts. The Legislature adopted the changes, which substantially increased the stakes for resort development on forest lands so that they would be at a scale that would mitigate against a proliferation of scattered urbanized enclaves of the type that Big Creek would have been. Although this opens the door to very large developments, it assures that there will be adequate financial investment to provide the necessary urban services. Raising the ante has resulted in fewer developments overall, and they have to be genuine resorts, with sufficient overnight accommodations and amenities—not a way of creating an urban development in a rural area.

The Supreme Court decision came down on March 19, 1984, remanding the Big Creek appeal to LUBA. Unfortunately for the resort opponents, Lane County's comprehensive plan had received its final approval by then. The Renaghans' changes had been adopted and were now part of the plan. Big Creek was zoned to allow a destination resort to be built on twenty-six acres in the northwest corner of the property. The rest remained Natural Resource/Prime Wildlife. Vic Renaghan signed an agreement with the Oregon Department of Fish and Wildlife as part of the conditions for the Forest exclusion (Goal 4), stating that he wouldn't build outside the commercial area reserved for the resort (other than systems for water, water treatment, sewage, and trails), something he had committed to during the West Lane Planning Commission hearings. This agreement became part of Exhibit B, the conditions that had to be met before the zone change became final.

Exhibit B also required a public hearing before the county signed off on the conditions, but no hearing was ever held. All conditions were supposed to be met, but some quite obviously weren't. Conditions pertaining to Big Creek Road, for example, were never met. The road was to be improved by flattening out the intersection with Highway 101, widening the road to sixty feet, and blacktopping the surface back to the east end of the property. The state highway department issued an opinion that the plans Renaghan submitted to deal with the road improvements would satisfy the Exhibit B requirements. They stipulated that no occupancy permit would be issued, however, until the improvements were completed. Thirty years later, the road is still gravel and meets Highway 101 on an awkward, pothole-ridden rise.

The Lane County Division of Land Use signed off and Vic Renaghan had apparently won the land use battles. Now he needed funding to actually build his resort.

CHAPTER FOURTEEN
THE INDUSTRIAL DEVELOPMENT BONDS

We were trying to be helpful as far as throwing sand in the gears where we could.

—Andy Kerr

On a mild, clear day in February 1984, Tom Smith stepped away from his workbench to stretch and flex his fingers, stiff from holding the chisel. He was carving a duck out of black walnut, enjoying the pleasure of creating something in three dimensions with his own hands. He'd met a lot of talented and artistic people since moving to the Oregon Coast, but only recently had he discovered woodcarving for himself. Sales of his carvings were a welcome contribution to the household income.

Working with hand tools—gouges and chisels—and only rarely using a small power drill, Tom carved ducks, and walking sticks, handrails and door panels. He could find a lot of exotic wood just by wandering down to the beach. Often he picked up agates and other stones to create necklaces made with the natural materials. The black walnut duck was going to be auctioned off at a fundraiser for Friends of the Oregon Coast planned for late April. He needed to do some more work on it—but he also needed to get out of the shop and feel the sun on his face. Tom walked across the highway to the parking area on the west side, where the Greyhound bus stopped and hitchhikers thumbed rides. The lineup of Tenmile mailboxes included some with colorful mandalas or psychedelic flowers. Others were rusted or looked like they'd been beaten with a two by four. Next to the mailboxes were tube-shaped receptacles for newspapers—green for *The Register-Guard*, orange for the *Siuslaw News*, yellow for *The Oregonian*.

It was the kind of day when people who live along the Oregon Coast allow themselves to hope that winter is over—but of course, there were still months of rain, wind, and fog to come. The heavy winter surf had piled up drift logs on the sand berm at the mouth of Tenmile Creek. A little more of the land along the bluffs had washed away. But on this day, the second-to-last day of February in the Leap Year of 1984, the constant susurration of the waves against the coarse gravelly sand was a source of meditative energy. Sunlight, just topping the ridge to the east, caught the white crests of the waves as they broke. Tom stood at the west edge of the parking lot, watching the water curling over, flowing back under the next wave, long lines of them breaking and retreating. He never tired of it. He considered walking down to the beach, but he needed to finish that duck, and by 2:30, he had to be in the driver's seat of the school bus, heading up to Yachats to bring the Tenmile kids home from school.

He pulled open his mailbox and shuffled through the usual bills and flyers, then pulled *The Register-Guard* out of its tube and went back to the house to make a cup of tea and scan the headlines before he returned to the shop.

"Big Creek" immediately jumped off the page. Larry Bacon, who covered news in the western part of Lane County for the paper, reported, "Developers of a proposed resort and convention center in the scenic Big Creek area along the coast, 14 miles north of here [Florence] are seeking $8 million in Oregon industrial revenue bonds."[210]

Tom forgot about the duck. He fired up the VW bus and headed up Tenmile Road to see Hans Radtke.

~

Earlier that month, the Big Creek LLC—Vic and Linda Renaghan and their partners, Estella and Peter Fuchs of Boca Raton, Florida— had submitted an application to the state Economic Development Department for $8.5 million in industrial development bonds (IDBs). Their request was on the Economic Development Commission's agenda for February, but it was withdrawn, according to Mark Huston, the manager of financing for the Economic Development Department at that time, in order to obtain the endorsement of the Lane County Board of Commissioners, a requirement of the state's IDB program.[211]

Originally estimated at $3.5 million, the costs of the Big Creek Resort had more than doubled, although Vic Renaghan said it might not cost as much as the $8 million dollars he was seeking. Part of the increase was due to the delays the developers had experienced, said Renaghan, but also he and his partners were now committed to "more of a world-class resort feeling." He said they were committing more resources to "basically the same thing."[212]

Actually, the plans had changed considerably.

Although still confined to the twenty-six acres in the northwest corner of the property—the only portion zoned DR for "destination resort" in the county's comprehensive plan—the Big Creek Resort project now included a 13,850 square-foot restaurant and conference center, a 3,000 square-foot tourist center, thirty cottages, two lodges containing a total of forty rooms, a recreation and exercise building, three tennis courts, a maintenance and craft center, and two houses that were intended for the Renaghans and their partners. Vic Renaghan and Peter Fuchs intended to be live-in managers.[213]

~

Tenmile Creek Road twisted along the side of the ridge, high above the creek. It was slow going, but Tom knew all the blind corners and tight curves from wrangling the school bus up and down the road. The Radtkes' house was west of Steve and Marie Cole's place, where the sauna was, although 1984 brought a lot of changes to the Tenmile community—some departures, some additions—and Leon Sterner and Caroline Bauman now lived in the old house where Steve and Marie had lived before. Fortunately, Leon and Caroline fit easily into the Tenmile community and the Sunday saunas had continued without a break when they moved in.

Hans and Karen Radtke were newcomers too. Several years earlier, Hans had been fishing on Tenmile Creek when he slipped and fell in. Dripping wet, he stopped at a restaurant in Yachats to dry off before driving back to Corvallis. Someone who worked there—the owner or a waitress, he couldn't remember—told him she was thinking of selling eighty acres about three miles up Tenmile. Hans called his wife.

"How much money do we have in our checking account?" he asked. She told him. "I just spent it all," he said. "I put a down payment on some property...."[214]

They cleared the property and built a house. Hans did some logging and ran cattle further up the valley; activities he later admitted were not the best thing for the environment. "But you do what you have to do to get by."[215]

He and Karen had met in Kali, Colombia—he was in the Peace Corps, and she, eager to get out of her native England, had moved to Kali to teach English. They returned to Oregon and Hans earned his Ph.D. in Resource Economics at Oregon State University, eventually working on his own as a freelance consultant. They raised two children and spent as much time as they could on Tenmile Creek until they were able to live there full-time. Karen taught school and worked at the Job Corps facility just north of Yachats, which had housed conscientious objectors during World War II. Eventually, they put the property in trust for their kids, with a conservation easement to protect the natural values.

After Tom told him about the development bonds, Hans requested a copy of the application from the Economic Development Department. He also arranged to meet with Robert Ackerman, an attorney in Eugene who, he'd heard, occasionally took on legal cases for free in the public interest.

~

Robert Ackerman was born in 1937 and grew up in San Francisco. At seventeen, he moved to Eugene to attend the University of Oregon. After he got his BA, he worked for several years until he could return to the University to get his law degree. His main practice was criminal law.

He was involved in politics and civil rights before he had any interest in ecology or the environment. When Eugene was exploding with anti-war and civil rights protests in the 1970s, he defended SDS, Students for a Democratic Society. He also defended members of the Black Panthers when no other lawyers would touch their high-profile cases. The Panthers weren't students; they came, he says, "because of the politics on campus." Panthers were "overcharged," he said—charged with murder, for example, when all they did was trespass. "The DA's office made mistakes," Ackerman added in a dry tone. Ackerman defended them, usually *pro bono*. "I was what you'd call a real liberal," he said.[216]

But it was with the lawsuit on behalf of ratepayers in Springfield, the working-class town across the river from Eugene, that he'd made his name, and the name of Peter DeFazio, who at that time was an aide to Congressman Jim Weaver. DeFazio had started looking into the commitment made by the Springfield Utility District to participate in the Washington Public Power Supply System's nuclear power plant construction program. WPPSS was in trouble by late 1981, and some utilities and individuals were beginning to question if they were going to get stuck with a massive bill regardless of whether the plants were ever built.

Robert Ackerman hated a boondoggle, and WPPSS was starting to look like one of the biggest boondoggles in history. By the summer of 1981, it was becoming clear that two of the plants, numbers 4 and 5, were never going to be built. A mutual acquaintance introduced DeFazio to Ackerman.

Ackerman didn't know if a lawsuit would accomplish anything. He wasn't a bond attorney; this was a brand new field for him. But he wanted to find out. "I was curious how ratepayers could be charged for something that would never be built," Ackerman said. "It seemed illogical, so I wanted to see if it was legal. And if it was, was it authorized?"[217]

After a careful review of the utility's contract with WPPSS, which took him "the better part of my spare time for two weeks," Ackerman concluded there was something wrong. He rushed to file suit against the Springfield Utility Board in order to "control the litigation from a ratepayer perspective."[218] Other ratepayers' suits were filed, some in the State of Washington. There were also suits by utilities, and outright refusals to pay what was due on the bonds.

Eventually, the Washington State Supreme Court issued an opinion on some of those utility suits, declaring that the utilities and their ratepayers were not liable for the WPPSS bonds. Although DeFazio and Ackerman lost in the early stages of their suit, the Oregon Supreme Court eventually overturned the initial ruling in their case. By that time, it didn't matter: Springfield and the other

Oregon utilities didn't have to pay. WPPSS would end up defaulting on the bonds, the largest public default in American history at that time.[219]

One of the results of the lawsuit, which was known as "the DeFazio case," was that it put Peter DeFazio's name before the voters in the Eugene-Springfield area. He ran for a seat on the Board of Commissioners, and was elected in 1983. His opposition to the Big Creek Resort, as a County Commissioner, and his later efforts as Congressman from Oregon's 4th District to find funding that would buy out the developer, would play a major role in the fight to preserve the Big Creek area from development.

~

After Hans Radtke contacted him, Robert Ackerman agreed to come to Florence for a meeting at the Bridgewater restaurant to discuss the issue with members of Friends of the Oregon Coast.

Driving over from Eugene, Ackerman didn't know if he was going to be representing two people or two hundred. He found a group of six people sitting in the back of the Bridgewater: Tom Smith, Jim Adler, Tony Cole, Bob Warren, Hans Radtke, and a young man from the Environmental Law Center of the University of Oregon who had heard about the Big Creek controversy and said he wanted to help. Billie Jo Smith and Ursula Adler stayed at the table where the group had eaten their lunch, on the other side of the restaurant.[220]

Tom described the reasons why Friends of the Oregon Coast was opposed to any development occurring at Big Creek: the endangered Silverspot Butterfly habitat, the use of the area by large herds of elk, the wild runs of salmon and trout in the creek. Bob Warren reported on the progress of the LUBA appeal. At this point, they were still hopeful that the Supreme Court would reverse the Oregon Court of Appeals decision that the appellants lacked standing to file with LUBA. That would send the issue back to LUBA, which would be forced to review the substance of the original appeal.

"What's the status of the development at this point?" Ackerman asked.

"So far," Tom reported, "not much has happened on the site."

Radtke thought it was possible that the developer didn't really expect to build, ever, that he was going through the motions with the expectation that he could sell the site once all the permits had been secured.[221]

Ackerman wanted to know if they had considered trying to buy him out. Tom said they didn't have access to that kind of funding. They talked about Vic Renaghan, his appearances at earlier hearings, his dismissive attitude about the "hippies" who were trying to stop his project.

Ackerman then explained what he and Hans were going to do. They would request all the documents filed with the application for the IDBs, including the Profit & Loss statement, depreciation schedules, projected payroll, tax filings by the principals, and so on. Hans Radtke would analyze the figures, and he and Ackerman would appear before the Economic Development Commission at the May 22 hearing. Neither would charge for their work.

Everyone approved. It was agreed that the objections would be filed in Tony Cole's name. Ackerman said he thought he could get Jerry Rust and Peter DeFazio to join the petition, since they'd objected to the Board of Commissioners' endorsement.

Tom rose from his seat, looking casually around the restaurant. Suddenly, he froze.

He bent down and whispered to Jim Adler, "Look over there." Jim followed the direction Tom was indicating. At a table near the front of the restaurant sat Vic Renaghan and his wife. Was this just a coincidence?

Renaghan looked up. He saw Ackerman and his face turned grim.

Why were the Renaghans there, at this particular restaurant at this moment? No one but the members of Friends of the Oregon Coast knew about the meeting.

Except... the student from the Environmental Law Center who had offered to help. He never showed up again and the suspicion was that he had tipped off the Renaghans, but nothing was ever proven.

~

The resort opponents kept up the pressure with public protests, letters in newspapers, and continued contacts with anyone they thought might be able to help. Before the Board of Commissioners hearing on April 12, at which the Commissioners would decide whether to endorse the application for the Industrial Revenue Bonds, about twenty-five people showed up to let the Commissioners know they were opposed to the funds being used to develop the resort, and that they wanted the Board of County Commissioners to refuse to approve the developers' application. They marched and sang, carrying posters that read, "No Tennis Courts on Big Creek," and "Only You Can Save Me," with a picture of a Silverspot Butterfly in the center.

Six people, including "coastal residents, environmentalists, and a state fish biologist"[222] spoke in opposition to the resort during the public comment period before the official meeting. Renaghan's attorney, Michael Farthing, and other people representing the developers, were there to answer questions from the Commissioners. Most likely, the demonstrations outside Harris Hall wouldn't have affected the vote, but in the end, it didn't matter—the decision to endorse the developers' application had been made before the demonstration began.

The vote was not unanimous however. Commissioners Rutherford and Rogers supported development of the resort. Rogers said that tourism was a great economic strategy because it would bring in "outside dollars" and have a multiplier effect since travelers attracted by a resort would spend money for meals, souvenirs, and other activities.[223]

Jerry Rust and Peter DeFazio voted against endorsing the bond application. Rust agreed tourism was good and it was fine to have resorts, but not at this location, where natural environmental values, such as the run of wild salmon, were more important. Accommodations would be better located in the towns of Florence to the south or Yachats to the north.[224]

DeFazio called the Renaghans' application "an abuse of the industrial development bonds," pointing out that the state bonds were intended to create high-paying jobs by building factories, not resorts that included residences for the owners and would provide only minimum wage service jobs.[225]

Commissioner Scott Lieuallen had voted for the zone change earlier, but he was having a problem with the Renaghans' application for the development bonds. Lieuallen was a strong supporter of liberal causes. As a member of the Eugene City Council, he had supported civil rights and gay rights, fought against the use of toxic herbicides, and promoted alternatives to car transportation, including expansion of mass transit in Lane County and building more bicycle-friendly facilities. Lieuallen practiced what he preached. He repaired bicycles for a living, and didn't drive a car. Being on the city council was a challenge; he was usually in a greasy t-shirt at work and didn't have time to change for meetings. He decided to run for the County Board of Commissioners. He lasted one term before his positions angered a lot of people and a poll showed he would never get re-elected.[226]

When I spoke to Lieuallen, he didn't remember voting for the bonds and was unhappy about his vote after I sent him the April 12, 1984 *Register-Guard* article about the Commissioners' decision.[227] At the time, he had thought that this wasn't an appropriate use of the state bonds, but he also felt that if Lane County didn't approve them and get the benefit of creating some jobs, some other county would, so he broke the tie. The application went on the agenda for the May 22 meeting of the Economic Development Commission.

~

Industrial development bonds, or IDBs, are referred to as "state bonds," but they are not actually issued by the state, nor does the state guarantee them. IDBs are a federal program that offers tax benefits to purchasers of the bonds for certain projects that have a public benefit. The states administer the program through issuing authorities such as state agencies, municipalities, counties, or port authorities that are responsible for making sure that projects meet the eligibility requirements of the Internal Revenue Code. Although the interest rate on IDBs is low, the bonds may be attractive to investors because the earnings are exempt from federal, and sometimes state, income tax.

The federal tax code was overhauled extensively in 1986, and some criteria that applied when the Big Creek LLC submitted its application for $8,075,000 in IDBs were changed. At that time, "certain tourism-related facilities" qualified, as well as manufacturing, processing, warehousing, research and development, and natural resource utilization. Now IDBs are specifically for manufacturing that provides public benefits through job creation, and projects such as solid waste disposal facilities that benefit the public by their function, i.e., waste disposal.

The Economic Development staff analyzed the Big Creek bond application and passed it on to the Economic Development Commission. The governor appoints people to the Commission from across the state who have financial expertise and other industry experience. (This function is now performed by a Finance Committee, also appointed by the governor.) The staff analysis would have taken into account the major public expenses that would be necessary to make the project viable.[228] The expenses would include the state and federal taxes that would not be paid because of the tax-exempt status of the bonds. They would also include any direct public expenses that, in the case of Big Creek, would have included road modification on Highway 101 to build a refuge lane for vehicles turning onto Big Creek Road, services such as school bus transportation for children of employees who might reside on the resort property, increased police and fire protection needs, and possibly transportation services for employees.

The staff analysis also would have included the public benefits such as taxable profits resulting from a successful new or expanded business and increased employment opportunities. New jobs generate revenues through payroll taxes and generally boost the economy with increased demands for housing, retail, and services in the location of the project. In an area as economically depressed as the Central Oregon Coast, a project that created new jobs—any jobs, even low-paying jobs—had great appeal.

Evaluation of IDB applications at the Economic Development Department is currently provided by Oregon4Biz staff. The key question in determining whether a project is cost effective is, "will there be sufficient tax revenue generated as a result of the project to offset the tax preference from the IDB?" Staff generally assumes that revenues generated by personal income tax will be sufficient to satisfy that requirement.[229]

Renaghan was confident the bond application would be approved. He expected to begin construction within five months, he told Larry Bacon, *The Register-Guard* reporter who had been covering the project. He "anticipated no trouble" finding investors to buy the bonds and characterized the opponents as "the same old opponents voicing a new type of opposition."[230]

~

The biggest selling point of the Big Creek Resort project was that it would bring much-needed jobs to the Central Oregon Coast. The Big Creek partnership had opened an office in Florence, managed by Shirley Hoggard, the new wife of the Reverend Robert Hoggard, to demonstrate a commitment to creating jobs in the community. They projected eighty-two new jobs resulting from the construction and operation of the resort. In the bond application, the total increase in payroll to investment was estimated at $803,700. However, Ackerman and Radtke's review of the application uncovered some inconsistencies.[231]

The payroll estimate was based on a 65 percent occupancy rate, but the gross income figure for the project was based on a 50 percent occupancy rate. Therefore, they pointed out, the application overstated the total increase in payroll due to the investment.

Also, the application didn't include payroll taxes for social security, unemployment, or workers compensation. These would have to be accounted for to provide an accurate estimate of the value of employment created.

The Big Creek LLC, with an operating history of less than one year, was required to include a three-year pro-forma balance sheet and monthly cash flow projections for a period of one year. Radtke and Ackerman were unable to obtain a profit and loss statement for the project. This meant there was no way to determine how the project would be depreciated, which would have "a substantial impact" on the taxable profits, which the developers projected to be $485,000 per year, starting with the first year of operation, although in their testimony, they also said they might run the project at a loss for the first three years.[232]

Another public benefit that justified issuance of IDBs was increased revenues to government from taxes. If the developers planned to take a loss in the first three years, the benefits they claimed as justification for the bonds would be "substantially reduced," according to Ackerman's testimony. If the losses were to be passed through to the investors, there would be a corresponding loss in federal and state income taxes, which would have an effect on the claim for public benefit as well.[233]

The analysis by the Economic Development staff failed to point out either the inconsistent occupancy figures or the possibility that the project would lose money in its first three years of operation.[234] There was no analysis of historic occupancy figures for coastal lodging properties, although travel on the coast is highly seasonal and many businesses suffer—some even close—during the off-season. Recent promotion efforts by TravelOregon, the state's tourism department, have focused on the so-called shoulder season—fall and late spring—in the hopes of off-setting some of those deficits, but at the time the Big Creek IDB application was being considered, shoulder season tourism promotion was not yet a significant part of state economic development efforts.

There were other flaws in the application. There was no breakdown of tax figures. The transient room tax, property tax, and personal property tax would all apply, and the amounts would vary depending on occupancy rates, appraised tax value, and the extent of personal property associated with the owners. None of this information was available.[235]

Ackerman was unable to obtain any figures regarding amortization of the bonds. The application appeared to indicate that some portion of the interest would be capitalized. Information about when the developers would be required to begin paying on the bonds and the amount of that payment would be critical, because it would affect the taxable profits.[236]

Although the state doesn't guarantee the bonds, they "have the state's name on them," according to a website on how to apply for IDBs.[237] The state is concerned about bonds being sold to people who don't understand the risk of the investment, people who aren't "sophisticated investors."

At the time of the Big Creek application, staff review was cursory at best, according to Ackerman and Radtke. Once staff had removed the two residences from the proposal and the Board of Commissioners had voted to endorse the application, it was very likely that the bonds would have been approved by the Economic Development Commission. Most such applications were approved, as a courtesy to local governments.

After Ackerman and Radtke testified at the Economic Development Commission hearing, Wayne Wolfe, one of the Commissioners, asked Ackerman to summarize his objections in a letter. Ackerman stated that the Commission staff review of this project was deficient. They accepted all of the figures provided by the developer without question, with the exception of the resident manager units, which they deleted. Ackerman wrote, "Since we have demonstrated that there is an internal inconsistency in the application and that certain cost factors have not been considered for the project, the staff report is inaccurate and will not support factual determination of the Commission that this project is eligible for industrial development revenue bonds."[238]

Applicants are advised in the department's instructions on filing that "financial statements submitted to the department are subject to public record law."[239] The department has some discretion about releasing some of the applicant's information, such as confidential reports obtained from "creditors, employers, customers, suppliers, financial statements, tax returns, business records, employment history and other person[al] data submitted by the applicant." Information that constitutes trade secrets is also protected. In a separate letter, Ackerman informed the Commission that he was filing a request under Oregon's open records law for disclosure of any additional information that was available to the Commission but not released to the public.[240]

Ackerman's earlier request for financial documentation submitted by Renaghan had been denied. Now he was asking again: How could the public evaluate whether IDBs should be issued if they couldn't obtain the relevant information? "The public is at a disadvantage," he wrote in his request, "when it does not have all the information that was available to your staff and to the Commission."[241]

He assured the EDC that he was not "anti-development." However, he and the petitioners he represented felt strongly that "the project should have financial integrity supported by documented information available to your staff and the public. That is the only basis upon which we believe an informed and reasoned judgment can be made regarding this application."[242]

After Robert Ackerman and I separately and repeatedly asked for the documents on the Renaghans' request, I was finally told that the records of the EDC hearing on the Big Creek project were no longer available. No decision was made at the May 22 meeting. The Commissioners were awaiting additional documentation, or testimony, plus, perhaps, a more thorough staff analysis. Renaghan didn't wait for that to happen. He withdrew his IDB application.

~

Renaghan was furious. He called Robert Ackerman and shouted that Ackerman had cost him $8 million dollars.[243] He also filed a complaint with the Oregon Bar Association against Ackerman, accusing him of soliciting business.

By the late 1970s, several legal cases had established that rules to curtail solicitation of business by lawyers constituted an unconstitutional violation of freedom of speech and association. One was *In re Primus*, decided May 30, 1978.[244] In that case, a lawyer in South Carolina, working with a branch of the American Civil Liberties Union, advised a group of women "of their legal rights resulting from their having been sterilized as a condition of receiving public medical assistance." The attorney then told one of the women "that free legal assistance was available from the ACLU." The lawyer was reprimanded under the State Supreme Court's Disciplinary Rules for soliciting business, but the federal court held that the state's disciplinary action violated the lawyer's rights under the First and Fourteenth Amendments. Ackerman cited *In re Primus* in response to Renaghan's complaint. The complaint was dismissed.

~

The Oregon Wilderness Coalition's contribution to the IDB controversy was to send a letter to the Internal Revenue Service Commissioner for Oregon, protesting that offering the tax-exempt bonds was a violation of the Endangered Species Act. This was another of Andy Kerr's bad boy actions, something he gleefully considers one of his more creative efforts on behalf of Big Creek. "Under the Endangered Species Act," he explained, "federal agencies must make sure that their actions do not jeopardize a listed species." If the IRS allowed borrowers to take a tax break on the bonds that were going to allow construction of a project that would harm the Silverspot without review and approval by U.S. Fish & Wildlife Service, they were in violation of the Endangered Species Act. Kerr admits that "to this day there is no case law whether that actually works or not. But it was one example where we were just trying to throw sand in the gears."[245]

One additional issue was left unresolved. The IDB application requires applicants to certify that, "no litigation is current, pending, or threatened in any court or other tribunal or competent jurisdiction, state or federal, in any way contesting, questioning or affecting the... ability of the applicant to complete the project...."[246]

Still pending was the LUBA case. The Oregon Supreme Court had sent the case back to LUBA. Tony Cole, Bob Warren, and the other appellants could now ask the Board of Commissioners to re-open the decision on the Renaghan zone change. The county's comprehensive plan had received its final approval from the Land Conservation and Development Commission, so the issue was essentially moot, but it left a shadow of uncertainty on the development.

Failure to obtain the state bonds was a serious blow to the Big Creek Resort project. It had now been over four years since the Renaghans bought the property and began the process of getting the permits and meeting the requirements of the zone change. They had very little to show for their efforts and potential investors were nervous about whether the resort would ever be built.

CHAPTER FIFTEEN
THE BUY-OUT

It couldn't change things. Killing one butterfly couldn't be that important! Could it?

—Ray Bradbury, *The Sound of Thunder*

...who knows what the Silverspot Butterfly means in terms of the ecology of the planet....

—Congressman Peter DeFazio, Big Creek video, YouTube

After Paul Engelmeyer and Mary Scully moved away from Tenmile, they lived in a house on the bluff north of Yachats. Finally, they were able to move back, buying a little house nestled in the spruce trees not far from the Stonefield-Smith house. Mary, a woodworker, did extensive remodeling and built a one-room cabin behind the house. On the east side of the house, a fence festooned with roses protected the vegetable garden from deer and elk. Paul and Mary had figured out how to grow a surprising variety of produce in a shady spot less than half a mile from the ocean. Paul managed the Audubon Sanctuary further up Tenmile Creek Road and worked with landowners and funding agencies to protect the forests of the Coast Range.

One day in 2005, the phone rang. Paul picked up.

"Vic Renaghan here. Let's talk."

Paul had waited almost twenty years for that phone call.[247]

~

During those two decades, Vic Renaghan kept trying to develop the Big Creek property while Friends of the Oregon Coast and their supporters tried to find ways to stop him. The Friends hoped from the beginning to solve the problem of a potential development by purchasing the property. Several times, they came heart-stoppingly close.

By 1989, Bob Warren, one of the founding members of Friends of the Oregon Coast and the named petitioner in the Friends' appeal to the Land Use Board of Appeals, was working for Peter DeFazio, who had recently been elected to Congress from Oregon's 4th District. Bob was in DeFazio's Eugene office when the receptionist buzzed him.

"Someone named Victor Renaghan to see you."

It must have been hard for Vic Renaghan to come to see him, Bob Warren speculated later. Bob was the lightning rod for all of Vic's problems with the Big Creek project. He was the face of the opposition. But here they were, both of them older and wiser and, in a sense, both on the same side.

Renaghan's question was... could Bob help find the money to buy Vic out?[248]

It seemed a likely possibility. Congressman DeFazio was on the Interior Appropriations Committee, a powerful position from which to push for funding from the Land and Water Conservation Fund. The Big Creek property would then become part of the Siuslaw National Forest. Renaghan was asking $2.5 million for the property. The money was there, as was a willing seller, but—the "buyer" balked. Forest Service rules required an appraisal and the appraisal determined the price. According to a memo from Bob Warren to Peter DeFazio, the bottleneck was the Review Appraiser in the Region 6 office of the Forest Service. In the late 1970s, this appraiser had been involved in an attempt by the Forest Service to acquire the Big Creek property. The property was then valued at $500,000. Why, he asked, should the Forest Service now pay five times as much for the same land?[249]

Vic Renaghan wasn't interested in half a million dollars. He believed his property, now zoned to permit commercial tourist use, was worth much more than that. The Forest Service wouldn't budge.

Bob Warren was outraged. "The money had been appropriated and it was for the greater public good," he said later.[250] He probably said worse at the time.

~

When Vic Renaghan needed an image for his Big Creek Resort letterhead, he chose the bowstring arch bridge that spans the creek to the west of the property, carrying traffic north and south along Highway 101. As an iconic image, it was a great choice for a logo—a graceful arch that frames a view of the ocean beyond. It's the same construction as the bridge over Tenmile Creek, where Tom Smith would often interrupt the family's dinner to rush everyone outside because the sun, setting behind the bridge, was putting on a spectacular show, each one the best ever, and not to be missed. Billowing clouds backlit by red and orange rays, or beams streaming through a hole in the clouds like a religious painting, or thick gray layers of rain-filled clouds edged with streaks of vermillion. Each sunset was the most gorgeous. Everyone had to see it. It got so annoying that Tom's oldest son, Rex, finally complained: "What kind of idiot compares sunsets?"

The Big Creek bridge was part of an ambitious state road-building program that began in 1917.[251] In 1919, following World

War I, Oregonians approved a referendum to build the Roosevelt Military Highway, eventually known as U.S. Highway 101, in order to be prepared for future emergencies. The state passed the first gas tax in the nation, a penny a gallon, to fund highway improvements. The Oregon State Highway Commission hired Conde McCullough, an engineering professor from the state agricultural college (later Oregon State University), as the state bridge engineer.

Robert Hadlow, in his book about Conde McCullough, *Elegant Arches, Soaring Spans*, writes, "Most people who hear McCullough's name will think first of the five major bridges that he designed for the Oregon Coast Highway during the first half of the 1930s. They are the pinnacle of his achievement as a designer, and a lasting monument to his contributions to the state... a culmination of years of studying and designing structures."[252] But even the smaller bridges, like Big Creek, Tenmile, and a third tied-arch bridge over the Wilson River in Tillamook County, were innovative. Based on "the tied-arch version of James Marsh's 'rainbow' bridge,' both in form and function," McCullough's designs "promoted economy without compromising modern highway traffic standards." They were also visually stunning.[253]

Construction of the Wilson River bridge began in the fall of 1930 and was completed in June 1931. Big Creek and Tenmile were completed by the end of 1931, for a cost of around $34,000 apiece. These weren't big streams—each channel was about 100 feet across—but the sandy bottoms meant McCullough couldn't construct abutment piers to hold the bridge in place. He dealt with this problem and other design constraints by using the tied-arch construction, in which the road deck functions like the string of a bow, "holding the outward thrust of the arch ribs in place through compression."[254]

By 1996, salt-laden marine air had corroded the structure of the Big Creek bridge. The Oregon Department of Transportation began the process of determining what to do—rebuild it or repair it. Bob Warren was now working as senior policy advisor for natural resources for Governor Barbara Roberts. One day he got a call from the Department of Transportation. Replacing the Big Creek bridge would cause a loss of wetlands. Could he recommend any mitigating action they could take?[255]

Indeed, he could. He recommended acquisition of part of the adjacent Big Creek property. If they could acquire enough acreage, it would stop the resort.

ODOT completed its "build/no build" study and decided to anodize the bridge supports rather than re-build the bridge. There would be no loss of wetlands to mitigate. Another opportunity to protect Big Creek vanished.

~

Tom Smith had made a commitment to saving Big Creek right after the County Commissioners reversed the West Lane Planning Commission decision. He told Billie Jo that he felt he had to do it. He knew how—networking, developing contacts, getting out information to key people, engaging people so they would get involved—and he had the time. Billie Jo was working full time. They didn't have much money, but they agreed to pay the phone bills—often more than $300 a month—and scrimp on other things. He was on the phone all the time, talking to different organizations, trying to get them to come on board to fight the resort development.

The Oregon Shores Conservation Coalition was founded in 1971 to protect the public interest in Oregon's beaches created by the Beach Bill.[256] Tom worked hard to get them to take a position against the resort. Although they had sent a letter to the West Lane Planning Commission opposing the Renaghans' request for a zone change, all that Tom could get from them during the County Commissioners' reconsideration of the request was a vote to stay neutral. He turned instead to the Oregon Wilderness Coalition, which became the Oregon Natural Resources Council, later Oregon Wild. Unlike Oregon Shores, which Tom felt was too political to take a strong stand,[257] Oregon Natural Resources Council was not afraid to ruffle a few feathers,

Tom joined the Wilderness Coalition board and eventually became the chair, traveling to Salem or Eugene for meetings, always looking for support to protect Big Creek, making phone calls, writing letters, strategizing. Along with Paul Engelmeyer, Jim Adler, and others, Tom monitored Renaghan's efforts to create development opportunities for himself or a potential buyer. They filed objections with the Lane County Planning Department, figuring that every delay bought a little more time to come up with the funds to buy the property and end any possibility of a development.

But in early 1990, Tom Smith faced an altogether different challenge.

There was a mole on his leg. He had a routine doctor's appointment scheduled three weeks after he noticed the mole and he figured he could wait until then to have it checked. During those three weeks, it grew. The doctor took a sample for a biopsy. The diagnosis was melanoma and surgery was scheduled. Through 1990 and 1991, there were two more surgeries. A staph infection followed one of the hospitalizations and proved impossible to cure.[258]

Billie Jo, a scientist to her fingertips, began researching treatment options. She discovered the Gerson Institute, and in October 1990, she and Tom traveled to Tijuana where he underwent treatment and she learned the complicated protocols to continue the regimen of juices, special foods, and cleanses like coffee enemas, which were supposed to flush out toxins in the liver and gall bladder. After a week, Tom's daughter, Stacy, flew down to learn the routines so that Billie Jo could go back to work. It seemed like some people at the clinic were getting better, Billie Jo recalled, "but Tom had already had so much chemotherapy at OHSU [Oregon Health and Science University] that his immune system couldn't begin to do the job."[259]

After Tom and Billie Jo returned from the Gerson Institute, the community rallied. People came in to prep vegetables for the juices that had to be made fresh and served every four hours, thirteen glasses of juice per day. Every week, Don and Blythe Collins Niskanen, who owned the New Morning Coffee House in Yachats, made a huge pot of the Gerson Institute soup, a careful blend of prescribed vegetables, and delivered it to the Tenmile house. Other people came over to make the juices, to bathe and groom Tom, to clean the house, and to make food for the family. Many came just to sit with this man who had been the center of the community for so many years.

Every now and then, Billie Jo would find a baggie of marijuana on the fireplace mantle. Tom was getting morphine and other drugs, she said, "but the marijuana seemed to be the only thing that really gave him relief from the nausea and pain."[260]

The Gerson regimen seemed to have a positive effect, Stacy recalled.[261] Tom's skin tone improved and his hair began to regain its normal color. But in spite of everyone's efforts, the cancer spread. By the fall of 1991, he couldn't leave his bed, which had been set up in the living room.

Thanksgiving had always been celebrated with enthusiasm in the community, first in the Smiths' living room, with tables stretched end to end from the kitchen to the front door. Then, when there were more people than the house could accommodate, the harvest dinner shifted to the old elementary school in Yachats where Billie Jo used to teach. After the school was closed, it had been purchased by the City of Yachats, becoming the Yachats

Commons, housing city offices and community meeting rooms. Ursula Adler, Marie Cole, Mila Niemi, and others decorated one of the former classrooms with sprays of fall leaves, moss and mushrooms, pumpkins and squashes. The men set up long tables that were covered with colorful Indian bedspreads. Turkeys were roasted in ovens all over town and people brought bean salads, green salads, pasta salads, fruit salads, casseroles of every type, and of course more than a dozen kinds of pie. Everyone was invited and everyone was welcome. For Thanksgiving 1991, more than sixty people were expected.

Tom decided not to go. He felt rotten, he couldn't eat, he couldn't walk. Stacy, exhausted from the demands of caring for her father and now in the early stages of pregnancy, agreed to stay home while everyone else headed up to Yachats.[262]

But on Thanksgiving morning, Tom decided he wanted to go. There was no wheelchair at Tenmile—when he had to go to the bathroom, someone "danced" him there, placing his feet on their feet, firmly but gently waltzing him from the living room to the bathroom. There was a mad scramble to find a wheelchair. One was located and someone drove to Yachats to pick it up. Tom, the wheelchair, and the Smiths' contribution to the feast were all loaded into the old camper and they headed up to the Commons.

It was Tom's last Thanksgiving. He died at home about 3 a.m. on December 24, 1991. His sons Rex and Ian, and son-in-law Chris Graamans, dug the grave in the woods above the house. They built the coffin and set it up in the living room. Billie Jo and Stacy washed Tom and dressed him in the Guatemalan robe he had worn to the sauna every Sunday for the past twelve years. By that afternoon, people began to arrive, crowding into the living room where he lay in his coffin. Blythe and Don's new baby, Robin, was passed over the coffin. She looked down and smiled at Tom. "One goes out and another comes in," someone murmured.[263]

There was a knock on the door.

The Lane County sheriff, who had often stopped by for a cup of coffee and a chat with Tom, stood on the porch, red-faced and awkward. Someone had reported that something was going on, that someone had died and was being buried on the property, unembalmed. He hated to bother them at a time like this, but he was required to follow up.[264]

Billie Jo came to the door with all the necessary papers and permits in a folder. The research on home burial had been done well before by one of Stacy's friends. Someone else drove to Florence to get the tags and paperwork done. An early morning call had brought Tom's doctor, Jerry Robbins, down from Newport to sign the death certificate.

It is perfectly legal to bury a body on private property in Oregon. You must own the property, you need written consent from the County Planning Commission, and you have to disclose the burials if you sell the property. (The Tenmile house is now in a family trust.) It's recommended that you draw a map showing the location of the gravesite and file it with the deed. The body must be buried within twenty-four hours of the death if no embalming takes place.

Alison Clement, her partner Chuck Willer, and their two children lived further up Tenmile Road. Alison is a writer and she wrote an essay about that day titled simply, "The Burial." She remembered it was a warm day, and it wasn't raining. She wrote about that last day with Tom—the gathering of people, the trip up to the gravesite.

The lid of the coffin was removed and people dropped flowers and small objects into the coffin and then the lid was nailed into place. "The hammering," Allison wrote, "was louder than anything you've ever heard."[265]

Billie Jo read selections from "The Gospel According to Shug," from Alice Walker's novel, *The Temple of My Familiar.*

"Helped are those too busy living to respond when they are wrongfully attacked: on their walks they shall find mysteries so intriguing as to distract them from every blow.

"Helped are those who find something in Creation to admire each and every hour. Their days will overflow with beauty and the darkest dungeon will offer gifts.

"Helped are those who love the stranger; in this they reflect the heart of the Creator.

"Helped are those who love the entire cosmos rather than their own tiny country, city, or farm, for to them will be shown the unbroken web of life and the meaning of infinity.

"Helped are those who laugh with a pure heart; theirs will be the company of the jolly righteous.

Helped are those who lose their fear of death; theirs is the power to envision the future in a blade of grass."[266]

The coffin went into the hole in the ground. The rich smell of forest soil rose up, dark and musky. Everyone stood around looking into that hole.[267]

Then something shifted. Alison remembers the sense of being present, totally and vividly alive "with all our senses, with every molecule." There was no eulogy. "The silence kept us out of our intellects," she wrote. "It kept us from creating a distance. We were just there, in the present, in our senses."[268]

It was Tom's final lesson—how to watch someone you love disappear into the ground forever.

There would be a big party at the Commons on New Year's Day, when the people who knew Tom Smith shared their stories and their memories, but during the burial, there was only silence. People thought about the ways Tom had touched their lives, hearing the big belly laugh, feeling his strong hands massaging necks in the sauna, remembering stories he told and people he helped, and every way in which he enriched the lives of the people around him, including, as Alison pointed out, showing them how to do death. He wasn't a saint and sometimes he was hard to live with, but no one who knew him would have missed any of it.

~

The Dunes Café in Florence was next to a laundromat at one end of a strip mall on the corner of Highway 101 and Highway 126. Paul Engelmeyer got a cup of coffee and sat down. Vic Renaghan came in a few minutes later.

They chatted briefly, establishing their positions, assessing each other. Finally, Paul told Vic he was here to do a deal. "We're committed to protection and restoration at Big Creek," he said. "We can find the money."[269]

Renaghan said he—his corporation—had put a lot into the property. There were some terrific sites for two homes with great views of the ocean and the Big Creek estuary. They were filing a Measure 37 claim, which would allow them to subdivide the property into fifteen 5 to 10-acre lots.

"It's not gonna happen, Vic."

"Is your defense guy still on it?" Renaghan asked. He was referring to Jim Adler, who had kept Vic's every move on his radar screen, filing the appropriate objections with the Lane County Planning Department.

"He is." Paul took a sip of his coffee and put the cup down firmly. "Listen, Vic. Your development is never going to happen. The opposition isn't going away. U.S. Fish & Wildlife has plans in place for habitat restoration for the Silverspot Butterfly. They don't want to see those efforts compromised with a big resort and houses all over the place. The Department of Fish & Wildlife doesn't want any new fishing pressure on the native fish in the creek, plus they're committed to maintaining elk habitat. All these agencies want to put management strategies into place to restore and preserve habitat. And we're on top of any land use moves you make. We're willing to work with you, but we need to know you're serious."

"How will you find the money?"

"Not a problem," Paul said. He had been successfully putting deals together to preserve land in the Coast Range. Now he unrolled his maps across the Formica table. "I've been doing land purchase agreements with the Forest Service, with Audubon, with State Parks. Here," he said, pointing to the map, "and here, and here."

"I don't want to work with the Forest Service," Renaghan said. "They're corrupt and they won't pay me what that property is worth. I could sell it, you know. Somebody wanting to put in a world-class resort...."

"Vic, look. The economy is slowing down. Did anyone make an offer on the property? You've had it listed for what? Five years? Did you get even one offer? Even Salishan is struggling."

"I want four-point-one million. It's worth it, all we put into it."

Patiently, Paul outlined the next steps. An appraisal had to be done and the price would depend on that. "Listen, Vic—The Nature Conservancy is interested in Big Creek. It's exactly the kind of project they could support. But I need to know you're serious. I need to go to them with a willing seller. You can't back away from this again."

Vic liked the idea of The Nature Conservancy. He thought they would be able to act faster than any government agency and could write him a check without a lot of time-consuming paperwork. He said he would take Paul's offer back to his corporation. Paul rolled up his maps. Vic put some money on the table for their coffee. They shook hands.

Paul went home and called Derek Johnson.

~

Ten years earlier, Derek Johnson was a young loan officer working for a mortgage company in San Diego. He wasn't saving the environment, which is where he'd anticipated having a career, but he was helping people and learning useful skills, and after all, he was in San Diego, where it was warm and sunny. Then a friend told him about a real estate position with The Nature Conservancy office in Wisconsin. He thought that sounded pretty good, so he left San Diego on a January day when the thermometer read 80 degrees, and got off the plane in Madison, where it was 32.

He met his wife there. They loved their jobs, the community, the friends they met, but in 2005, a job opened at The Nature Conservancy office in Portland, Oregon. Portland was on their short list. He applied and got the job. One of his first assignments was to visit the Central Coast and meet Paul Engelmeyer.

Paul gives great tours. His passion sings out: protect this wetland, restore this Coho stream, create a new park for people to explore the beauty of the coastal forest, make sure there are still some trees left. He and Derek went to the Audubon Sanctuary on Tenmile Creek, a serene meadow canopied with huge old river maples. The Oregon Department of Fish & Wildlife and the Forest Service had recently completed a project there, helicoptering big logs into the stream to slow the flow and provide deep pools and places where gravel would accumulate, enhancing the chances of Coho eggs surviving to hatch.

And Paul took Derek to Big Creek.

Derek remembered Paul saying that this was the number one property. He ticked off fifteen reasons why. "It was just like blazed in my brain," Derek said. "It all made sense to me."[270]

Paul told Derek that the owner lived in Hawai'i, but that he came over to the mainland occasionally. "You should try to connect with him."

~

Meanwhile, the Renaghans and their lawyer, Michael Farthing, were busy trying to realize some value from the Big Creek property. Although three site plans were prepared and submitted to the Lane County Planning Department, nothing was ever built. Lack of funding was a major obstacle, one that Vic Renaghan believed was due to the actions of Planning Department personnel and the "malicious" challenge to his IDB application.

Efforts to develop at least some part of the property focused on two strategies. One strategy was to build two houses, what Renaghan called either a "watchman's cabin" or a "caretaker's dwelling." The idea was that he or someone else could live there and monitor trespass and other violations on the property. Both dwellings were outside the twenty-six acres zoned Destination Resort, which was the only part of the 186 acres where development could take place. In addition to protocols to protect Silverspot Butterfly habitat, Renaghan had signed an agreement with the Oregon Department of Fish & Wildlife intended to prevent human impact on what was significant elk habitat. Other than infrastructure such as the water and sewage disposal systems, and trails for guests of the resort, the major part of the property was off limits to construction.

During this time, Friends of the Oregon Coast closely followed all planning decisions involving the Big Creek property. Other agencies and organizations also filed objections, particularly to applications for building houses on the property outside the resort zone. At different times, both Renaghan and the resort opponents were convinced that the planning department staff was not on their side, which seems to indicate that there was no consistent bias toward either party. Planning Director Kent Howe corroborated that view. "It's not the business of planning staff to decide whether a project is good or bad," he said. "Their job is simply to apply the law, and that's what they did."[271]

~

The other strategy was to partition the property into two or possibly three parcels that could be sold, perhaps to raise cash for the resort development. In 1991, the Renaghans applied to partition the property and create a buildable lot on the ridge south of the creek. Their application was denied on several grounds. There was no way to access the south side of the property because most of the land between Big Creek Road and Renaghan's proposed partitioned lot was an estuary zone. Since the State Highway Department would not approve an approach permit onto Highway 101, there would have to be a bridge across Big Creek and the wetlands. The Highway Department memo noted, "the state is having trouble repairing the Hwy bridge due to the estuary zone," which made it very unlikely that Renaghan could get a permit for another bridge across the wetlands. The same interoffice memo, dated February 5, 1991, concludes that the whole discussion is probably irrelevant since "I think he used this area as part of the area to remain undisturbed so he could get the Destination Resort zoning north of Big Creek Road."[272] This was a continuing theme for most of the decisions about the Big Creek property. Renaghan and his lawyer claimed that they never agreed to forego development on the property outside the Destination Resort zone; the opposition, supported by several different agencies, insisted that they had.

The District Wildlife Biologist at the Department of Fish & Wildlife, Gary Hostick, told the Lane County Planning Director, "We are opposed to this partition," noting that the area is "designated major big game range, and is used by elk." Elk habitat would not be compatible with any additional building construction in the area. "If dwellings must be constructed," Hostick wrote, "minimum lot size recommended is 80 acres."[273]

The basis of the objection was the Exception determination that allowed the zone change from Prime Wildlife to Destination Resort.

During the hearing on the Renaghans' request for the changes that would allow them to build the resort of their dreams, Renaghan had said he had no intention of building in the Prime Wildlife zone. Eventually, he signed an agreement with the Department of Fish & Wildlife as a condition of the county's finding of an Exception to the existing Natural Resource (NR) zone. The agreement with Fish & Wildlife was an integral part of the zone change, required to meet Statewide Planning Goal #4 to protect and preserve forestlands. Changing the twenty-six acres where the resort would be located to Destination Resort (DR) was an Exception justified by potential economic growth. It was offset by maintaining all of the property not zoned DR as habitat. Renaghan's attorney, Michael Farthing, claimed that the Exception did not apply outside the DR zone, and therefore the agreement with Fish & Wildlife wouldn't apply either. Or conversely, perhaps it did apply but that didn't mean that no development could occur outside the DR zone.[274]

The planning director, Michael Copely, held that the Exception pertained to the entire 186 acres, not just the DR zone. The property was considered a "single integrated unit," all of it part of tax lot 300. This essentially meant that no development could take place on the remaining 160 acres, zoned NR, Natural Resource.[275]

The 55 acres south of Big Creek Road could be construed as a separate legal lot because zoning regulations regard roads as dividing lines. This is what happened on Tenmile when the MacCraes' 320-acre property was divided into several smaller parcels after the Coles bought it, because of the way the road ran through the property. Planning Director Copely found that the smaller parcel "is a separate legal lot and can be separately conveyed and possibly developed pursuant to zoning restrictions."[276] However, that didn't change the underlying Comprehensive Plan designation and zoning regulations, nor did it solve access problems across the estuary and wetlands.

Farthing also said in his memo that the NR zone was not adopted to protect forestland (based on soils analysis and other conditions listed under Goal #4), but to "protect the property from development that might be inconsistent with surrounding public ownerships and natural resource features." He said that the proposed partition wouldn't affect the public land surrounding the Big Creek site, nor would the location of homes on the lots "have any adverse impact upon the use and enjoyment of those public lands by visitors to this section of the coast."[277] These statements may have been true, but that was not the reason for the NR zone exclusion of development to which Renaghan had agreed.

Renaghan claimed that the trees on the DR parcel were "deformed,"[278] wind-blown shore pine and spruce with no timber value. That part of the property is buffeted by salt-laden wind and has thin soils, both of which create less than ideal conditions for Douglas-fir and other trees that could be harvested as timber. But a good deal of the property is timbered—and it's elk habitat, which is the main focus of the agreement with Fish & Wildlife that Renaghan had signed in order to satisfy the conditions of Exhibit B before he could get a use permit for the resort. [279] In addition, the west portion of the north ridge, where Renaghan was proposing to create another buildable lot, was potential Silverspot Butterfly habitat.

Farthing acknowledged that there were several statements in the Findings and Exception adopted in 1981 and readopted in 1984 that suggest no development could occur on or in the Natural Resource zone but "there was nothing that prohibited partition of the property outside the DR zone." The intention to protect the "natural resource values of the site" really applied to protection of sensitive areas, he claimed, which meant the Big Creek estuary, the elk habitat area, and Silverspot habitat. None of these areas, Farthing claimed, would be impacted by the partition since "no development is proposed to be located within any of those areas."[280]

The lawyer also argued that single-family dwellings are special uses in the NR zone. Such uses require approval by the planning director or a hearings officer. Since there is provision for approval, it could be assumed that the use is not denied out of hand

Farthing acknowledged that staff at the Department of Land Conservation and Development (DLCD) had told him that the circumstances of the adoption of the Exception as a condition for the intense level of development for the resort and the County's decision not to apply Goal 8 and designate areas of the County as suitable for destination resort development meant that "the exception may still have vitality."

Nonetheless, Farthing continued to maintain that the "Exception is limited to the twenty-six-acre parcel designated Destination Resort." If it did extend beyond, it was to protect "unique and natural resource areas." He and Renaghan continued to argue that because the partition wouldn't affect any such areas, the NR restrictions were irrelevant.[281]

The argument seems convoluted and confusing, but the planning staff continued to maintain that the Goal 4 Exception applied to the whole property outside the DR zone, not just the timbered areas. The planning director maintained his denial of the partition and a hearing was set for June 13, 1991. The staff report recommended that the Hearings Official uphold the Director's decision to deny the partition request.

~

According to Matt Spangler, now the Senior Coastal Policy Analyst with the Department of Land Conservation and Development and formerly Planning Director for Lincoln County, developers do not get a return on their investment by building a resort facility like the one that Renaghan initially proposed for Big Creek, with a lodge, some cabins, a "trading post," and restaurant. They make money by selling real estate—residential lots on which people build homes, as primary or secondary residences.[282]

Revisions to Statewide Goal 8 had changed the need for finding an Exception in order to approve a destination resort on rural forestlands. Counties were to inventory potential sites for destination resorts, opening the door to construction, but only under certain restrictions. Large destination resorts—the Salishans and Sun Rivers of the future—could include residential development but they were required to provide two units of overnight accommodations for every one residential unit and the kinds of amenities commonly associated with destination resorts, such as golf courses or tennis courts.

Smaller developments were for overnight accommodations only. Although it seemed counterintuitive, the idea was to make the bar to large-scale developments so high that only a very few would be feasible and that they would be genuine destination resorts, not an excuse for urbanized development in a rural area. This meant there would be far fewer "scatterations," Tom McCall's descriptive word for pockets of urbanization in what should remain productive farms or forest. Lane County, like many other counties with potential destination resort sites on rural lands, hadn't undertaken the Goal 8 inventory process.

Did Renaghan intend to develop a residential subdivision? In a twelve-page memo addressed to the Hearings Officer in November 1992, Renaghan focused first on the two managers' houses, which he said had been in the plan from the beginning. Then he talked about "just a handful of compatible homes in that relatively huge acreage." Eventually he discussed his objections to a statement by county staff that "once built, all units in the resort had to be sold all at once or not at all." This would contravene "any lawful and traditional private property rights for unit sales to recover capital... and [was] in contravention to LCDC's written DR testimony and ruling that such DR units could be sold with lots after buildout."[283] Clearly, this refers to more than just the owners' residences or cabin accommodations for guests of the resort.

There was also confusion about what a "unit" was—was Renaghan planning to build cabins? Or triplexes to be rented or sold as condo units? Or home sites where people would build houses they would then own and presumably be able to sell as individual units? When the resort needed to show transient rental income, each of the thirty buildings was described as three rentable units. When fewer "units" were needed to meet the land use requirements, the three were condensed back into one.

The partition hearing was postponed to August 1, 1991 at Renaghan's request.

~

By November, the hearings officer had not yet reached a decision about the partition. Michael Farthing forwarded to the planning director Renaghan's lengthy memo arguing for approval of the partition application. He noted in his letter, "Mr. Renaghan has expended a considerable amount of time in preparing a chronological review of the planning process which resulted in the current NR and DR zoning and plan designations for the subject property."[284]

More than anything, the memo reveals Vic Renaghan's extreme frustration regarding the Big Creek property. He claims that he and his partners had always intended to build the two residences to live in, separate from the resort itself. If the resort were sold, that didn't mean the homes would also be sold, although elsewhere he maintains that they'd have every right to sell the homes. He said that the site plan showed the location of the residences and that it had been available for public review as part of the "Intent to Rezone." The residences had always been proposed as "a private property enclosed residence (a mini-estate concept) providing an effective trespass barrier and guardianship or 'husbandry' of the land between the relatively intensive DR use and adjacent public lands," (underlining in original document).[285]

Referring to the Board of Commissioners' "Findings of Fact and Conclusions of Law Supporting Approval of Plan Amendment and Zone Change," Renaghan points out that the two owners' residences are included in the document and that the applicant was found to have addressed all the Statewide Goals. The zone change findings say that NR zoning "is intended to protect the majority of the property from activities which could destroy or degrade the scenic values, natural areas, or wildlife habitat of the Property." Renaghan believed the entire NR zone was intended to be a "transition between the development area and the adjacent Rock Creek Roadless Area (now designated Wilderness), 'Retention' lands and Washburne State Park."[286] The memo also mentioned that at some point in this process, the Renaghans had had discussions with The Nature Conservancy about putting the property into a conservation reserve.[287]

The findings that supported the zone change, Renaghan insisted, were "defended by us, in behalf of Lane County." Renaghan claimed that they took the fight right up to the State Court of Appeals "which upheld the findings."[288] In fact, the "fight" didn't stop with the Court of Appeals. It went all the way to the State Supreme Court, which found only that the appellants—Bob Warren, Tony Cole, and the others who filed the LUBA appeal— had standing to appeal. The courts didn't actually deal with any substantive issues.

There are some other odd misstatements in the memo, including a reference to the application for Industrial Development Bonds (IDBs). Renaghan states that the application was approved by the County Commissioners, with the two residences included.

That is true, but the next statement, "We were approved for $7.8 million in IDRBs for the balance of improvements in the NR zone plus the full DR construction,"[289] is misleading. Even if the Economic Development Commission had approved the application, the residences were specifically eliminated from the expenses that could be covered by the bonds. The application itself was withdrawn following Robert Ackerman's testimony based on Hans Radtke's economic analysis.

Renaghan remained extremely unhappy about his dealings with Lane County. He claims in the memo that opinions expressed by the staff in response to inquiries by potential investors and buyers, "have driven these folks away from financial participation or purchase of Big Creek Resort or its associated property."[290] Eventually, he would conclude that the state of Oregon, Lane County staff, and Peter DeFazio in particular, were all corrupt, by which he meant that they followed their own personal values rather than policies adopted through democratic processes.[291]

In conclusion, Renaghan argued, "...there must be an end to the County staff's incessant re-definition and drastic re-qualifications of issues pertaining solely to this project." He concluded his comments with his personal philosophy:

"In human affairs, the economic usage of land is, in a very practical sense, as important as the sensitive use of it for the benefit of all God's creatures. That same environment must be protected by people sensitive enough to realize that 'leaving things alone' may be counterproductive to the salvation of all species (such as the Silverspot Butterfly, elk, fish and Man). In the long run, enlightened protection brings personal satisfaction. The profit aspect allows us the means to survive to fulfill the ideas that will bring credit to man, nature, the Government, and our Country in general."[292]

~

As 1992 rolled around to 1993, the management plan with the Department of Fish & Wildlife continued to be the key issue. Renaghan acknowledged that he had signed the agreement, but claimed that it was not yet in effect. He said that they had taken numerous actions to improve elk habitat, working with Bob Vincent, a wildlife biologist, including the creation of "a permanent elk forage area on eleven acres of meadow between Big Creek and the County Road."[293]

Renaghan claimed that a letter to the Planning Department regarding the partition, written by Jim Adler (who continued to receive and respond to all notices pertaining to the Big Creek development), suggests that the management agreement with ODFW required them to "surrender our property to the exclusive use of ODFW."[294] That, of course, is not what the agreement proposes, nor, according to Adler, is that what he said in his letter.[295]

"This type of allegation, and badgering public agencies and officials who grant us our legal rights," Renaghan continued, "is a 'friends' [meaning, presumably, Friends of the Oregon Coast] tactic designed to confuse, confound and weaken the resolve of those responsible for administering the law, and has contributed to great confusion during the lengthy, multiple hearings processes we have undergone to gain the right to use our private property lawfully and responsibly."[296]

Adler wrote in one of his letters to the Planning Department that the Department of Fish & Wildlife agreement was part of a bargain, an exchange to balance the intense development in the DR zone.[297] That statement is supported by the mildly worded Director's opinion regarding the partition application: Renaghan's proposed partition "constitutes a form of development on property committed by the Exception to non-development."[298] The Director added, "Numerous statements are made (in the Exception) committing the NR (Natural Resource) area to an undeveloped condition in exchange for intensive development of the DR (Destination Resort) core area."[299]

Renaghan was incensed. "To suggest that our leading edge of environmental concern in development was done to 'bargain' with any agency is unfair to the agencies involved, misleading in intent, and untrue."[300]

Renaghan tried to claim that there was a shift from Forest to Natural Resource, but Natural Resource was the zone designation when Renaghan bought the property. The zoning did not shift to NR to prevent "rapacious clear-cut logging," as Renaghan claims. In fact, "rapacious clear-cut logging" was perfectly permissible (assuming compliance with Department of Forestry rules) before the change to DR/NR, and would still have been permitted if he had not signed the Exception agreement with the Department of Fish & Wildlife.

Renaghan continued to maintain that no reasonable landowner would, in exchange for the development rights in the DR zone, have ever allowed an agency such as the Department of Fish & Wildlife to "exclude us from use of our own land."[301]

Of course, they were not excluded from the land, but their use was limited. The agreement allowed infrastructure outside the Destination Resort zone to support the resort, and some construction of trails for the use of guests. Nothing in the agreement was intended to keep guests from rambling through the woods.

Renaghan's memo concluded that if the agreement meant what the Department of Fish & Wildlife and the planning staff said it meant, "we would have simply granted the land to ODFW and not spent our labor, worry, months of our lives, tens of thousands of dollars in wildlife enhancement and protection actions, and paid years of taxes on the land."[302]

On August 2, 1993, Vic Renaghan notified the Hearings Officer that he was withdrawing his application for the partition of the Big

Creek property. He had decided that this was the only way to move forward with plans to develop the resort, because the "Land Management Division has taken the position it will not process any application for site plan approval until the partition appeal has been resolved."[303]

~

In 1994, Victor Renaghan, as Managing Partner of the Big Creek Limited Partnership, filed a General Land Use Application to build a 170-unit "Destination Health Resort," on the twenty-six acres of his property that was zoned DR, Destination Resort. Phil Martinson Engineering Inc. was listed as the agent. Martinson's firm prepared the site plan using the old name for the area, Roosevelt Beach Resort. The plan anticipated construction of thirty-four duplex units situated along twenty-foot-wide roadways, a sixty-unit "Primary Hotel Building," a forty-two-unit "Isolated Luxury Hotel Building," a health spa, gift shop, recreation center, "Convention/ Restaurant/Shop Building," and "associated amenities."

A membrane bio-reactor would treat wastewater to a level that could be used for irrigation and fire suppression. Road improvements, including refuge lanes to manage traffic on Highway 101, would be constructed with input from the Oregon Department of Transportation (ODOT). The resort layout is roughly parallel to the existing Big Creek Road, extending up the hillside onto a bench of semi-flat land.[304] However, no construction was begun.

Meanwhile, Renaghan retired from his job with the U.S. Customs Service. It appeared that he didn't have the funds to develop the Big Creek property and he hadn't found a buyer. He tried a number of tactics to realize something from the property.

One strategy was to apply for legal lot verification. Keir Miller, who began working for Lane County Planning around that time, explained that a property owner could research the deed history of a property to see if there was a possibility of creating legal buildable lots without going through a formal subdivision.

"People did a lot of things with older properties," Miller said. "Parts were deeded off, there were conveyances, parts could be sold and resold" even though it was all one owner.[305]

Looking at the old property records, it's not hard to see how that sort of confused history might occur. The land that Amel Stonefield owned went to his wife Marie when he died. It included the 186 acres that the Renaghans bought, but that wasn't all of it. Marguerite Sherwood deeded part of the property to her husband Hugh "for love and affection" after they married, though there was nothing in the deed records to identify who Marguerite was or how the property came into her possession. Other parts of the original Stonefield property were sold or deeded to other parties—the Forest Service, the State of Oregon (for road construction), even The Nature Conservancy.

A legal lot verification, also called a "seed lot," was very controversial and contrary to state planning policies. But even before SB 100 and the adoption of the county's comprehensive plan, the NR—Natural Resource—zone was in place on the Big Creek property and was intended to discourage subdivision and development. "It's a very restrictive zone,"[306] Keir Miller explained, and it included all of the Renaghans' property that surrounded the twenty-six acres where the Big Creek resort would be built. Even without the agreement with the Department of Fish & Wildlife, it would have been impossible to build more than one house.

~

As the twentieth century came to an end, Oregon's land use laws were fully grounded into the state's landscape. All the county comprehensive plans were in place to meet the nineteen goals that had been developed by an extensive public process. Governor McCall had declared that land use planning was about more than "preserving the beauty of Oregon." It was critical for ordinary people to be involved in determining how the economy should grow in a "sane manner." In typical grand McCall fashion, he added, "In short, we're talking about People and the Land."[307] Citizen participation was Goal One of Oregon's Land Use Goals: "To develop a citizen involvement program that insures the opportunity for citizens to be involved in all phases of the planning process."[308]

The Land Conservation and Development Commission had eleven months to come up with statewide planning goals. Boldly, they had committed to a public involvement program that eventually drew in more than three thousand people to workshops all around the state. The Commission worked especially hard to encourage participation outside Oregon's urbanized areas. Surveys showed that although participants weren't typical Oregonians— they were better educated, owned their own homes, had relatively high incomes, and were two-thirds male—they were also not affiliated "with groups or organizations involved in land use issues."[309]

Nonetheless, there were always opponents, particularly in the timber and real estate sectors. There had been a couple of earlier efforts to repeal or modify the state's land use laws, but none was successful. In 2004, however, a group called Oregonians in Action collected enough signatures to get another measure on the ballot to restrict land use regulations.

Measure 37 was titled "Governments must pay owners, or forgo enforcement when certain land use restrictions reduce property value." If passed, it would require compensation to be paid to property owners whose property values were reduced because of land use regulations. Qualified owners would need to file a demand for compensation equal to the reduction in fair market value of the affected property. In lieu of payments, which would clearly outstrip the ability of local governments to pay, the owners would be allowed to turn back the clock to a time when the restrictive zoning did not exist.

The proponents of Measure 37 ran a smart, emotional campaign. The Voters Pamphlet for the 2004 election in Oregon was full of stories of people who couldn't re-build after their home burned down, who couldn't subdivide and sell their property to support their retirement, who were told, "a home for a fish is more important than a home for your family."[310]

"Oregon's land use laws," said another supporter, "are stealing the life savings from Oregon's seniors."[311]

Measure 37 supporters quoted the Bible. "Private property is one of the most basic freedoms spoken of in the Bible. The 8th Commandment prohibits theft. The case laws in Exodus 21-23 require restitution to owners of property stolen or damaged by others. Deuteronomy 27:17."[312]

The campaign was full of appealing stories of "ordinary Oregonians" whose God-given right to do what they wanted with their property had been totally compromised. And not only the deity, but the Constitution of the United States gave people rights that the State of Oregon was trampling on. The Fifth Amendment to the Constitution states, "...nor shall private property be taken for public use, without just compensation." Under the theory of eminent domain, governments could appropriate private land for public purposes, but the owner of that land must be compensated. The land use laws were portrayed as a regulatory taking, creating harm to people who once had a right to do something on their property that they were now prohibited from doing.

The poster child for the Measure 37 campaign was Dorothy English, a woman in her nineties who wanted to pass her land on to her kids when she died. Her property was rezoned as forestland and could no longer be subdivided. The campaign hit a responsive chord with many Oregonians. "That's not the way things are done in this country,"[313] declared one statement. "Measure 37 will make sure that property owners are treated fairly, and that no one is forced to give his land to the state for free."[314]

Opponents of the initiative were emotional too. They feared that every rural property in the state would be covered with five-acre lots, the fulfillment of McCall's dire warnings about the spread of urban development destroying the beauty of the state. But Tom McCall was no longer around to rally his fellow Oregonians. (Tom McCall died in January 1983.) The opponents of Measure 37 considered a campaign that would feature images of every iconic location in the state covered with shopping malls, parking lots, and ticky-tacky houses. Instead, they rationally pointed out that Measure 37 would cost the taxpayers of the state $344 million just to administer, before anyone received a single dollar for a claim.[315] Hearts were not moved.

There were other arguments, of course. The League of Women Voters' statement predicted that Oregon would end up just like all those other states where quality of life was compromised by unmanaged growth. The American Institute of Architects claimed that Measure 37 would create "economic windfalls for a few large landowners while taxpayers foot the bill... Large timber, mining, and development interests will be released from protecting the environment while the rest of us face higher taxes, instability, and uncertainty."[316] But abstractions about land use laws couldn't compete with an elderly woman who just wanted to give something to her grandchildren before she died. As the election returns came in that night from Portland precincts, Measure 37 was running even, pro and con. This was not a good sign. Without a strong margin of "no" votes from liberal urban voters, the measure could win.

And win it did—61 to 39 percent.

Measure 37 became law as ORS 197 352 (2005). By March 12, 2007, 7,562 Measure 37 claims covering 750,898 acres had been filed in Oregon.[317] Vic Renaghan filed his Measure 37 claim for the Big Creek property on September 29, 2006. Faced with the deluge of claims, most counties simply approved them. On March 20, 2007, the Lane County Board of Commissioners passed his claim, along with a batch of others. This turned the clock back to the zoning that existed when he bought the property, which was Natural Resource with Prime Wildlife Overlay. It was, as Derek Johnson of The Nature Conservancy put it, an attempt to "supersize the resort."[318]

But actually, the Destination Resort zone, which he had applied for and appealed to the Board of County Commissioners after the West Lane Planning Commission turned him down, was gone. As the property owner, Renaghan could carve his 186 acres into fifteen parcels of five- to ten-acres each and sell them as home sites.

What was he thinking?

For one thing, he apparently was thinking that his property was now worth around four million dollars. Dale Saari, a broker with Windemere Realty in Florence, and Michael Smith of Windermere West Coast Properties, met with Renaghan at Big Creek. In a letter to Renaghan dated April 22, 2006, Saari provided an evaluation of "your proposed sale of six ocean view lots on the south side of Big Creek, ranging in size from 5 to 10 acres."[319]

Saari estimated the value of each property at between $350,000 and $400,000. These were view lots along the ridge south of the creek, facing the ocean. A similar value would also "pertain to the other ocean view properties you own on the north side of Big Creek, regardless of lot size... A two-acre parcel with an excellent ocean view will sell for as much as a several-acre parcel, especially if the topography of the smaller parcel is better for accommodating a home and outbuildings."[320]

On the other hand, developing these parcels was not simple. Saari told Renaghan as they walked over the property that each lot had to be "legally created through Lane County."[321] Septic systems for each parcel, water, electric, and other utilities, and a paved road that would meet county standards for access by fire-fighting equipment would all be required. The Department of Transportation still had not signed off on an access road to the south end of the property from Highway 101, and a bridge across the creek would have been expensive, even assuming he could get permission to build it. Without waiting for a permit, Renaghan had a crude road bulldozed along the south ridge facing the ocean. It wasn't paved, and would not have met county standards for emergency equipment access, and the highway access permit was still necessary.

In other words, there would be substantial costs to develop the property, which is something other Measure 37 claimants were discovering. The zoning may have reverted to the time when the claimant purchased or inherited the property, but health and safety requirements did not. Those requirements were the main line of defense against the anticipated subdividing of the state.

If he was unable to develop buildable lots for single-family residences, Renaghan could still sell "ocean view camp lots that would probably sell in the $15,000 to $20,000 range," Saari told him, cautioning that county restrictions on the amount of time a camper may remain on a lot might reduce the value even more.[322]

~

After discussions had begun with The Nature Conservancy, and after Renaghan had filed his Measure 37 claim, he was still trying to do something with the property. Once again, he pushed to build houses that he referred to as caretaker or "watchman" cottages where he, or someone, could live and keep watch over the property.

He claimed that people were trespassing, camping illegally, killing elk out of season, even dynamiting the river to kill salmon. He saw the caretakers' cottages as an essential part of a wildlife management plan, although the county planning staff insisted that management plans and watchman's cottages were generally aspects of nonprofit ownership of a protected area. As the department understood the term, there was no management plan.

When he came to the Planning Department with plans for a caretaker's cottage, the staff was dubious. It looked as if Renaghan's plan was to get one dwelling on the property, sell it, and then have money to proceed with the other lots. As Lane County Planner Keir Miller said, "The watchman cabin didn't meet the straight-face test."[323]

Nonetheless, Miller and fellow planner Steve Hopkins went to the Big Creek property do a site assessment. They walked up to a clearing on the north side of the property. Renaghan was proposing to put the "cabin" in the middle of the field. It was a beautiful site, but in terms of providing a vantage point for monitoring vandalism, it didn't work very well. Most of the area where people camped was not visible from the site, though it did have a good view of the ocean.

Also, the site Renaghan had chosen for his caretaker cottage was clearly identifiable as Silverspot habitat. "It wasn't wise... if you were planning to protect and do habitat restoration," said Miller. "That was our take and we recommended denial."[324]

Miller remembers that Vic Renaghan was "spinning out lots of ideas—what he was envisioning, what his goal was. He had some law enforcement background," Miller recalls, "but he said he wouldn't carry a gun." Miller recalls Renaghan saying, "I use my mind. I talk to people, that's what I'm good at."

While he was on the property with Keir Miller and Steve Hopkins, Renaghan told them he was going to confront the trespassers who were camped there. He exuded confidence, Miller recalls. He went up to the trespassers and told them to leave. They did.[325]

A biologist from the Portland U.S. Fish & Wildlife Service office also attended the site visit. She arrived first and parked her car on the old logging road on the north side of the property. She was there to provide an evaluation on whether the site was in fact Silverspot habitat. Renaghan pulled his car in behind her, blocking her in.[326]

"We had never done butterfly surveys on this property," the biologist recalled, "but it was adjacent to the Rock Creek butterfly population." She thought it was possible this might be butterfly habitat.

Silverspot numbers were crashing on the Rock Creek Forest Service property. In 2005, there were fifty-five butterflies. The next year only half that number. U.S. Fish & Wildlife Service decided to release captive-raised butterflies from the Portland Zoo to see if the butterfly population numbers would go back up.

If requested, a biologist would conduct a site visit to see if an area looked like butterfly habitat. Most of the time it wasn't, but this open patch on the north side of the Big Creek property, where Renaghan planned to build one of the "watchman" cottages, looked like a possible site. It was January. The plants were still dormant, so the biologist couldn't determine if there were violets on the meadow, but it looked like typical *Viola adunca* habitat.

Renaghan was treated "like any other landowner," the biologist said. He needed to get a letter saying his construction plans wouldn't hurt the listed species before he could get a building permit. U.S. Fish & Wildlife never said he couldn't build. They would make a series of recommendations for actions that would protect the habitat. One was to do a violet survey in the spring "to see if it was really habitat or not." Renaghan declined the offer to do a violet survey on his property.

The conversation grew increasingly intense. Renaghan recalled his past frustrations with the Forest Service, his "neighbor" to the north. He believed the property lines had been moved, reducing the size of his property.

It began to get late and the biologist felt increasingly uncomfortable. After the owners' spouses told Renaghan to "let her go," he moved his car so she could leave. She decided to request additional support when attending future meetings with Renaghan.[327]

About six months later, another U.S. Fish & Wildlife employee had a field meeting with Renaghan. The Silverspots had hatched and were definitely present on the site. In fact, the biologist caught one in his hat and showed it to Renaghan.

Renaghan continued to follow his own logic in where he planned to build. He wrote his own habitat management plan for the butterfly, which was determined by the U.S. Fish & Wildlife biologists to have no scientific merit.[328]

~

In 2007, the Oregon Legislature placed Measure 49 on the ballot to correct some of the damaging effects of Measure 37. Sixty-two percent of the voters supported it. Claims were now to be filed with the Department of Land Conservation & Development, rather than each county. The number of houses that could be built on high-value farmland and forestland by any claimant was reduced to no more than three. This gave some satisfaction to the Dorothy Englishes of the world, but precluded large-scale rural subdivisions on farm- and forest-zoned land, thus preserving the intent of SB 100.

Renaghan filed a Measure 49 claim with the Department of Land Conservation & Development, requesting a supplemental review of his Measure 37 claim. If approved, he would be allowed to create up to three home sites. By November 30, 2009, however, Victor Renaghan was no longer the owner of the Big Creek property. His request for relief under Measure 49 was therefore denied.[329]

In late 2007 or early 2008, The Nature Conservancy and the Renaghans had begun discussing the sale of the Big Creek property. After some back and forth via email, Renaghan called to say he really wanted to talk about selling the property. He and his wife Linda met with Derek Johnson and other Nature Conservancy staff at Zell's Café, located around the corner from The Nature Conservancy offices in Portland. The discussion continued in The Nature Conservancy conference room.[330]

Renaghan described his history with the property, including his Measure 37 claim. He believed his property was worth a lot of money, around five million, as Derek recalled. Renaghan said it was a turnkey property, ready to be developed. It was the only spot in Lane County legally zoned for resort development. He gave Derek all the papers, including his Measure 37 application and the subsequent Measure 49 application. "It was, literally, a book," Derek told me when we began talking about the Big Creek history. Then Derek delivered the heartbreaking news that all those documents were gone, recently tossed into the recycling bin.[331]

Renaghan talked and talked, Derek remembered. He claimed that not only was the property worth the money he was asking for it, but he had a potential buyer. Derek wasn't taken in. He thought that if Renaghan had someone that excited about buying the property, he'd be talking to them, but here he was, talking to The Nature Conservancy. "Let's get the appraisal done," Derek said, "and see what it's worth. If that's its value, let's sign it up and see if we can find a way to pay for it."[332]

They drew up a Purchase and Sale Contract. "I did what's called a Range or Floor/Ceiling approach," Derek said. If the appraisal comes in at less than the seller's minimum, he can walk. If it's more, The Nature Conservancy could walk because they can't pay more than the appraised value. "If the appraisal is somewhere in between, then we've got a deal."[333]

The floor was $4.25M. The appraisal was difficult, with the resort zoning and the Measure 37 and 49 claims. A firm in Eugene that The Nature Conservancy had worked with on their similarly challenging Willamette Confluence project did the appraisal, which came in at $4.07M. Derek had to ask Renaghan to drop down. "He didn't really hesitate very much," Derek said.[334]

The process for The Nature Conservancy to buy a piece of property is fairly complex, increasingly so the greater the dollar amount involved. The Big Creek acquisition was funded with money from a revolving fund managed by The Nature Conservancy's main office in Arlington, Virginia. Basically, they have created their own bank. Local offices like the one in Portland borrow from the fund and are obligated to repay the money. The Big Creek project was approved by the Oregon Nature Conservancy advisory board and then by The Nature Conservancy's Presidential Review Committee, which consists of four or five people representing conservation, government relations, and finance. They review the transaction, looking at the values of the project, how the money will be paid back, and how the reputation of The Nature Conservancy might be affected. "Of course," Derek Johnson said, "there's always a lawyer on the phone making sure we're following all the rules."[335]

After the sale closed, Derek and other Nature Conservancy staff needed to find an appropriate owner of the Big Creek property. "We call it a co-op project where we're stepping in and owning for a short period and then deed it over," usually to a public agency like the Forest Service, Derek explained. Meanwhile, they started searching for the money to pay back the funds they'd borrowed from The Nature Conservancy's revolving fund. "We put a lot of irons in the fire," Derek said.[336] Not everything went as planned.

They began by applying for grants from the Oregon Watershed Enhancement Board, U.S. Fish & Wildlife Service, and the National Oceanic Atmospheric Administration's Coastal and Estuarine Land Conservation Program, respectively referred to as NOAA and CELCP, pronounced 'kelp.' They also considered the Forest Service. If they could bring the value down through other grants, perhaps the Forest Service would be willing to buy in and incorporate the Big Creek property into the Siuslaw National Forest.

The Forest Service idea fell apart almost immediately because of the involvement of the Watershed Enhancement Board as a potential funder. The state agency provides grants to help communities and individuals improve water quality and protect salmon habitat. The agency is funded from the Oregon Lottery, federal dollars, and salmon license plate revenue. When they provide a grant for land acquisition, it almost always comes with a strict conservation easement to protect their investment and make sure stream conditions won't be compromised by future activity.

Aside from the politically charged legal question about a state agency imposing conditions on a federal agency, the Forest Service doesn't want any third-party encumbrances on title to land that they own, which is what they'd have if Watershed Enhancement money was used. The state money cancelled out the Federal money, end of story. With populations of native trout and salmon in Big Creek, the Watershed Enhancement Board was a natural partner, but the easement requirement pretty much ruled out Forest Service ownership.

Derek didn't lose any sleep over including the Forest Service in the Big Creek buy-out plans. The Oregon Watershed Enhancement Board agreed to a two million dollar grant, which was one of the biggest grants they had approved at that time. Derek was now halfway to the $4.05M goal.

A grant application to the U.S. Fish & Wildlife's Recovery Land Acquisition (RLA) program for $1M was approved, but again there were problems with the delicate balance of deciding which pot of federal money would work best in the mix. RLA had some concerns and Derek decided to put that application on hold while he pursued the CELCP grant, which was a highly competitive program. CELCP is able to fund only seven or eight of the more than fifty project applications they receive each year. The Nature Conservancy's first application for Big Creek bounced up against a change in program rules that gave a certain percentage of the grants to the National Estuarine Research Reserves program. The second year, they failed to address the issue of "threat" and just missed the cut-off.

Threat refers to the potential for adverse effects on the property. Derek laughed ruefully when he explained the CELCP grant saga. The Nature Conservancy needed to make the case that even though they now owned the property and were not about to build a destination resort on Silverspot Butterfly habitat, there was still a threat to that habitat. Fortunately, they had help—first from NOAA, which really wanted to fund the Big Creek purchase, and then from the state Department of Land Conservation and Development, which helps administer the CELCP funds. The agencies coached The Nature Conservancy on a better way to answer the threat question, and on their third try, they were approved for $600,000.

CELCP funds can't go to a nonprofit, which is why the Department of Land Conservation and Development was involved. They actually apply for the grant and then "subgrant" the money to another agency. In the Big Creek case, the agency was the Oregon Parks & Recreation Department, which then transferred the money to The Nature Conservancy to pay back their funds.

Life is not simple in the world of grants, especially when real estate is involved. The Nature Conservancy bought the Big Creek property just before the 2008 crash in real estate values. By the time they had the property re-appraised for the CELCP grant, the value had dropped. Agencies are bound by appraised values. Instead of $1.2M, which was the amount CELCP had approved, State Parks could only take half that amount.

No one knew the crash would be as bad as it was, or that it would last as long as it did. "It was a bit of a risk," Derek admitted, but even if they might have bought the property for less, it wasn't worth the risk of losing the deal. "We're in the business of preservation," he added, "not in the business of making money." The Big Creek funding pressure was compounded by The Nature Conservancy having a couple of other big acquisitions pending in Oregon—at Table Rocks and Hells Canyon—totaling around $12M. They lost "a couple million" in depreciation, and the economic downturn also affected philanthropic donations, but in the end, they did it. Big Creek was protected and the loans were paid off. By 2015, Derek said, The Nature Conservancy was "completely current and moving along."[337]

In spite of the economy, loyal supporters stood by the organization. Several hundred thousand dollars were raised specifically for Big Creek. It must have been dear to the hearts of these donors. In September 2013, when the celebration was finally held at the Cape Perpetua Visitor Center to mark the transfer of the property to State Parks, representatives from the agencies—the Department of Fish & Wildlife, the Forest Service, State Parks, U.S. Fish & Wildlife, and some of the other individuals whose persistence had kept Big Creek from being developed—came up to speak and share their memories of the long struggle.

Two people no one seemed to know stood off to the side, watching. I asked Paul Engelmeyer who they were. He didn't know their names, only that they had donated a considerable sum of money to The Nature Conservancy for Big Creek.

Mary Scully, Paul's wife, asked, "But who are they?"

"You know the guys from ODFW?"

Mary nodded.

"And Michelle Jones from the Waldport office of the Forest Service? And Bob Warren? And Bob Ackerman?" Paul named several other people and Mary and I both acknowledged that we knew who they were.

"Well," he said, "the couple standing off to the side who you don't know? That's who they are."[338]

They have chosen to remain anonymous. Who they are and why they supported the Big Creek acquisition so generously remains a mystery.

~

On September 13, 2013, the people and agencies who had persisted for nearly forty years to save Big Creek and keep it in its natural condition celebrated their hard-won success. Bob Warren brought a flyer for one of the spaghetti dinner fundraisers. Robert Ackerman spoke softly about how he hated a boondoggle. Billie Jo Smith presented framed photographs of the Big Creek bridge and estuary taken by well-known photographer Scott Blackman—one to Jim Adler, one to Paul Engelmeyer, the 'bad cop/good cop' routine that had kept the cause going during the past twenty years since the court cases and land use decisions had been made. The brothers Pip and Tony Cole, who had cabins up Big Creek, were there, and of course people from The Nature Conservancy. After the speeches and the credits, everyone sipped white wine, ate ceviche, and looked down at the ocean seething in and out of the Devil's Churn far below.

The work of preserving Big Creek continues. Management plans are in place to deal with Silverspot habitat and the invasion of

Japanese knotweed. Agency cooperation is essential—Oregon Department of Fish and Wildlife, the Siuslaw National Forest, U.S. Fish & Wildlife Service, State Parks, and The Nature Conservancy all have a stake in how the area is managed, and there are areas of disagreement even though the end goals are very close.

The terms of the transfer to State Parks stipulate that there will be no development at Big Creek other than (perhaps) a trail connection from Washburne State Park on the south to the Rock Creek Wilderness on the north. At present, there are no specific plans for such a trail. There are a few signs explaining that the acquisition was made possible by The Nature Conservancy. Other signs notify hunters that there is no hunting on State Park property. Boulders have been rolled into place to prevent people from driving down to the river and camping.

~

Congressman Peter DeFazio had supported efforts to protect the Big Creek property for nearly four decades. Unfortunately, he was unable to attend the Cape Perpetua event on September 13. A special celebration had been arranged at the Big Creek estuary on August 20, to acknowledge his support. Michael Dennis from The Nature Conservancy did a quick review of the strange history of the Big Creek property, from the proposed nuclear power plant, to the destination resort. "For decades," he said, "people knew we had to protect this place."[339]

Debbie Pickering, who manages Silverspot habitat for The Nature Conservancy, also put the Big Creek acquisition in historical perspective. "From 1943 to 2005," she said, "over one hundred acres of coastal prairie habitat in the general vicinity [of Big Creek] has been lost. Working with partner organizations, The Nature Conservancy has helped restore habitat while also supporting local jobs," she said.[340]

After he accepted a framed photo of the estuary from Billie Jo Smith, Congressman DeFazio talked about how important it is for humans to work to prevent the extinction of species. Thinking of the frustration, now twenty years in the past, of not being able to use Federal dollars to add Big Creek to the Siuslaw National Forest, he smiled and said that he hoped "someday we'll spend the Land and Water Conservation Fund for land and water conservation!"[341]

~

That evening, the community gathered at Hans and Karen Radtke's house on Tenmile Road. As the last bits of baked salmon were nibbled out of the pan and the last lettuce leaves were lifted from various salad bowls, the Earth turned and the light faded as the sun disappeared behind the ridge on the south side of the Tenmile Creek drainage. The air immediately cooled and people reached for fleece, shrugged into Pendleton plaids, slipped a green University of Oregon or orange Oregon State sweatshirt over their heads. It was still light; the Oregon twilight would last until nearly eight on this September evening. Murmuring conversations went on across the tables, recollections, stories, lies. Another bottle of wine was opened. Someone laughed.

Gradually people began clearing the food away, packing up the leftovers. Someone grabbed one last brownie off a tray. The bottles were collected for recycling, the paper and plastic separated, the garbage put in a bear-proof can. Young couples carried sleepy children out to their cars. Now in their twenties and thirties, most of the young parents weren't even born when the Renaghans' zone change application came up before the West Lane Planning Commission back in 1981.

In twos and threes, the Silverspots fluttered over the table. The spots on the undersides of their wings gleamed against the fading cinnamon-brown color. They were battered and tired, wild animals approaching the end of their brief lives, seeking shelter among the trees. Their status under the Endangered Species Act played an important role in fortifying the determination of the local community and the funding agencies to save Big Creek, to protect the salt-spray meadows and try to assure the survival of the Oregon Silverspot on the coast.

Congressman DeFazio had mentioned the Silverspots in his comments on August 20, saying that we never know exactly what role any given species might play in the ecology of the world.[342]

The Butterfly Effect comes to mind.

The Butterfly Effect is a meme that refers to chaos theory—the scientific notion that so many unknowns can affect outcomes that they aren't always predictable, although its evolution in popular culture has taken it to mean—incorrectly—the opposite, that if we know about small events, such as the flutter of a butterfly's wings over the Pacific Ocean, we will be able to predict a hurricane in the Caribbean.

While creating a weather simulation program in 1961, MIT meteorologist Edward Lorenz discovered that a small change—rounding off a decimal figure—caused unexpected shifts in the outcome. Over time, the divergence increased exponentially until the outcome was far from what his original input had predicted. When he published a study of this phenomenon, titled "Deterministic Nonperiodic Flow," a colleague commented that one flap of a seagull's wings could change weather predictions. By 1972, when Lorenz delivered a paper at a conference of the American Association for the Advancement of Science, the title had morphed to the more enticing, "Does the flap of a butterfly's wings in Brazil set off a tornado in Texas?"[343]

When Tom Smith first saw the Big Creek Resort sign, who could have known that the fate of the property would be affected by the listing of a butterfly as a threatened species?

Although Ray Bradbury's short story, "A Sound of Thunder," was written in 1952, long before Lorenz's discovery, it also relies on a small, seemingly insignificant event in the past to explain momentous change far in the future. And, coincidentally, it is the death of a butterfly that causes the changes over time that result in a very different world.[344]

The story involves Eckles, a hunter on a time travel safari. The year is 2055 and a new president has just been elected, a decent person who defeated Deutscher, the fascist candidate. The hunters enter a time machine and are transported back 65 million years to the Cretaceous Period. Their quarry is a Tyrannosaurus Rex who will be killed by a falling tree after they shoot him, so they're not changing anything. They are warned repeatedly not to step off the special elevated path, not to touch anything, definitely not to shoot anything unless directed by the guides. But Eckles panics and steps off the path. When the party returns to the safari office, nothing is quite right. The language has changed, colors are subtly different— and Deutscher has won the election. Eckles looks at the bottom of his boot. There is a crushed, dead butterfly in the mud he picked up when he stepped off the path.

Over the thirty-five years of battling to stop the development of a destination resort on the Big Creek property, so many things could have gone wrong and prevented the success of the campaign. The Silverspot might not have been listed. The Industrial Development Bonds might have been approved. At the most basic level, people might have grown weary of paying attention. But people persevered and the natural values of Big Creek were saved.

~

The celebratory gathering ended and people left the Radtkes' house, the headlights of their cars flashing in and out among the trees as they wound their way down the twisting gravel road. Four miles south, Big Creek flowed through the wetlands, under Conde McCullough's bridge, and out into the Pacific. Ground fog rose among the willows and sedges. The trees stood their ground as the last light faded away. It was dark then, and quiet, a night without the lights or noise of human habitation, the last undeveloped place on the Central Oregon Coast.

APPENDIX A
OREGON'S STATEWIDE PLANNING GOALS

GOAL ONE: CITIZEN INVOLVEMENT

Goal 1 calls for "the opportunity for citizens to be involved in all phases of the planning process." It requires each city and county to have a citizen involvement program containing six components specified in the goal. It also requires local governments to have a committee for citizen involvement (CCI) to monitor and encourage public participation in planning.

GOAL TWO: LAND USE PLANNING

Goal 2 outlines the basic procedures of Oregon's statewide planning program. It says that land use decisions are to be made in accordance with a comprehensive plan, and that suitable "implementation ordinances" to put the plan's policies into effect must be adopted. It requires that plans be based on "factual information"; that local plans and ordinances be coordinated with those of other jurisdictions and agencies; and that plans be reviewed periodically and amended as needed. Goal 2 also contains standards for taking exceptions to statewide goals. An exception may be taken when a statewide goal cannot or should not be applied to a particular area or situation.

GOAL THREE: AGRICULTURAL LANDS

Goal 3 defines "agricultural lands." It requires counties to inventory such lands and to "preserve and maintain" them through farm zoning. Details on the uses allowed in farm zones are found in ORS Chapter 215 and in Oregon Administrative Rules, Chapter 660, Division 33.

GOAL FOUR: FOREST LANDS

Goal 4 defines forest lands and requires counties to inventory them and adopt policies and ordinances that will "conserve forest lands for forest uses."

GOAL FIVE: OPEN SPACES, SCENIC AND HISTORIC AREAS AND NATURAL RESOURCES

Goal 5 covers more than a dozen natural and cultural resources, such as wildlife habitats and wetlands. It establishes a process for each resource to be inventoried and evaluated. If a resource or site is found to be significant, a local government has three policy choices: preserve the resource, allow proposed uses that conflict with it, or strike some sort of a balance between the resource and the uses that would conflict with it.

GOAL SIX: AIR, WATER AND LAND RESOURCES QUALITY

Goal 6 requires local comprehensive plans and implementing measures to be consistent with state and federal regulations on matters such as groundwater pollution.

GOAL SEVEN: AREAS SUBJECT TO NATURAL DISASTERS AND HAZARDS

Goal 7 deals with development in places subject to natural hazards, such as floods or landslides. It requires that jurisdictions apply "appropriate safeguards" (floodplain zoning for example) when planning for development there.

GOAL EIGHT: RECREATION NEEDS

Goal 8 calls for each community to evaluate its areas and facilities for recreation and develop plans to deal with the projected demand for them. It also sets forth detailed standards for expedited siting of destination resorts.

GOAL NINE: ECONOMY OF THE STATE

Goal 9 calls for diversification and improvement of the economy. It asks communities to inventory commercial and industrial lands, project future needs for such lands, and to plan and zone enough land to meet those needs.

GOAL TEN: HOUSING

Goal 10 specifies that each city must plan for and accommodate needed housing types, such as multifamily and manufactured housing. It requires each city to inventory its buildable residential lands, project future needs for such lands, and plan and zone enough buildable land to meet those needs. It also prohibits local plans from discriminating against needed housing types.

GOAL ELEVEN: PUBLIC FACILITIES AND SERVICES

Goal 11 calls for efficient planning of public services such as sewers, water, law enforcement, and fire protection. The goal's central concept is that public services should to be planned in accordance with a community's needs and capacities rather than be forced to respond to development as it occurs.

GOAL TWELVE: TRANSPORTATION

Goal 12 aims to provide "a safe, convenient, and economic transportation system." It asks that communities address the needs of the "transportation disadvantaged."

GOAL THIRTEEN: ENERGY

Goal 13 declares that, "land and uses developed on the land shall be managed and controlled so as to maximize the conservation of all forms of energy, based upon sound economic principles."

GOAL FOURTEEN: URBANIZATION

Goal 14 requires cities to estimate future growth and needs for land and then plan and zone enough land to meet those needs. It calls for each city to establish an "urban growth boundary" (UGB) to "identify and separate urbanizable land from rural land." It specifies seven factors that must be considered in drawing up a UGB. It also lists four criteria to be applied when undeveloped land within a UGB is to be converted to urban uses.

GOAL FIFTEEN: WILLAMETTE GREENWAY

Goal 15 sets forth procedures for administering the 300 miles of greenway that protects the Willamette River.

GOAL SIXTEEN: ESTUARINE RESOURCES

Goal 16 requires local governments to classify Oregon's 22 major estuaries in four categories: natural, conservation, shallow-draft development, and deep-draft development. It then describes types of land uses and activities that are permissible in those "management units."

GOAL SEVENTEEN: COASTAL SHORELANDS

Goal 17 defines a planning area bounded by the ocean beaches on the west and the coast highway (State Route 101) on the east. It specifies how certain types of land and resources there are to be managed. Major marshes, for example, are to be protected. Sites best suited for unique coastal land uses (port facilities, for example) are reserved for "water dependent" or "water related" uses.

GOAL EIGHTEEN: BEACHES AND DUNES

Goal 18 sets planning standards for development on various types of dunes. It prohibits residential development on beaches and active foredunes, but allows some other types of development if they meet key criteria. The goal also deals with dune grading, groundwater drawdown in dunal aquifers, and the breaching of foredunes.

GOAL NINETEEN: OCEAN RESOURCES

Goal 19 aims "to conserve the long-term values, benefits, and natural resources of the nearshore ocean and the continental shelf." It deals with matters such as dumping of dredge spoils and discharging of waste products into the open sea. Goal 19's main requirements are for state agencies rather than cities and counties

INTERVIEWS

In addition to research in primary source documents, books, and articles on various subjects, *Saving Big Creek* has relied on interviews with numerous people who were involved in one way or another with the Big Creek property, including members of the "Greater Tenmile community," academics, professionals, staff of various agencies and organizations, and many others. Grateful thanks to all the people listed below. Any errors or misinterpretations are mine alone.

Robert Ackerman, attorney
Jim Adler, member, Friends of the Oregon Coast
Ursula Adler, weaver, Yachats River resident
Sy Adler, Professor of Urban Planning, Portland State University
Caroline Bauman, Tenmile resident
Jesse Beers, Cultural Director, CTCLUSI
Karen Bennett, Hydrologist, U.S. Forest Service
Nathan Buehler, Communications and Marketing Manager, Business
    Oregon
Ed and Charlotte Chaney, former National Wildlife Federation
    employees
Marie Cole, Tenmile resident
Pip Cole, Big Creek resident
Tony Cole, Big Creek resident
C.J. Drake, Georgia-Pacific
Paul Engelmeyer, environmental activist, Tenmile resident
Jerome Garger, Yachats resident

Russ Hoeflich, Executive Director, The Nature Conservancy, Portland

Kent Howe, Planning Director (ret), Lane County

Jim Jackson, Adjunct Professor of Geology, Portland State University

Derek Johnson, The Nature Conservancy

Andy Kerr, environmental activist, member Oregon Wilderness Coalition

Cameron LaFollette, executive director, Oregon Coast Association (ORCA)

Scott Lieuallen, former Lane County Commissioner

David McCorkle, professor of biology (ret), Western Oregon University

Marnie McPhee, writer

Keir Miller, planner, Lane County

James Montieth, Executive Director (ret), Oregon Wilderness Coalition

DJ Novgrod, Realtor, Yachats OR

Debbie Pickering, Oregon Coast Ecologist, The Nature Conservancy

Shirley Plummer, poet, former wife of Tom Smith

Hans and Karen Radtke, Tenmile residents

Victor Renaghan, owner of Big Creek property, 1979-2008

Lance Robertson, public affairs, Eugene Water & Electric Board (EWEB)

Jerry Rust, former Lane County Commissioner

Sarah Scholfield, Tenmile resident

Mary Scully, Tenmile resident, woodworker

Timothy Sercombe, Justice, Oregon Court of Appeals (ret)

Jack Sleeper, Fisheries and Aquatic Biologist, U.S. Forest Service

Billie Jo Smith, educator, wife of Tom Smith

Ian Smith, son of Tom Smith

Stacy Smith, daughter of Tom Smith

Matt Spangler, former director of planning for Lincoln County, now Senior Coastal Policy Analyst, South Coast office, Department of Land Conservation and Development (DLCD)

Phyllis Steeves, archaeologist on the Siuslaw National Forest (ret)

Leon Sterner, Tenmile resident

Anne Walker, Biologist, U.S. Fish & Wildlife Service

Bob Warren, environmental activist, member Friends of the Oregon Coast

Chuck Willer, environmental activist, Tenmile resident

Doug and Susanna Beck Yunker, "Little Corvallis" residents

BIBLIOGRAPHY

_____ "Big Creek: A Coastal Gem," *This Year in Oregon Annual Report 2009*, The Nature Conservancy, p. 9.

_____ Endangered Species Act of 1973 (Wikipedia)

Adler, Sy, *Oregon Plans: The Making of an Unquiet Land-Use Revolution*, Oregon State University Press, Corvallis, Oregon, 2012.

Alt, David; Donald W. Hyndman; *Northwest Exposures: A Geologic Story of the Northwest;* Mountain Press Publishing Company; 1995.

Atwood, Brian, and David Yamaguchi, *The Orphan Tsunami of 1700: Japanese Clues to a Parent Earthquake in North America,* University of Washington Press, January 1, 2005

Bacon, Larry, "Big Creek seeks state aid; opponents get court review," *The Register-Guard,* February 28, 1984.

Baldwin, Lew, "Ten Mile woodcarver appreciates coastal lifestyle," Newport *News-Times,* February 3, 1988.

Barnes, John, *The History of Carl G. Washburne Memorial State Park*, self-published, undated.

Beck, Mary F., *The Ten Mile Story,* self-published, 1972.

Bernstein Litowitz Berger & Grossmann, LLP, Cases, Case Number 88-md-0551, History of Class Action Suit Against WPPSS, 2014.

Bogue, Barbara Beck, *Proved Up on Ten Mile Creek: The Story of the Early Settlers of Ten Mile Creek, Oregon, 1986,* compiled by Susanna Beck Yunker, self-published, 1991.

Bishop, Ellen Morris, *In Search of Ancient Oregon: A Geological and Natural History;* Timber Press; 2003.

Bishop, Ellen Morris, *Living With Thunder: Exploring the Geologic Past,*

Present, and Future of the Pacific Northwest, Oregon State University Press, 2014.

Bradbury, Ray, "A Sound of Thunder," 1952.

Brown, Mary Lou, "Pro—Con: Should a Multi-Million Dollar Resort Be Built in This Undeveloped Coastal Area?" *Oregon Coast,* June/July 1982.

Chasan, Daniel Jack, *The Fall of the House of WPPSS,* Sasquatch Publishing, Seattle WA, 1985.

Cole, Tuna, Pip Cole & Crew, *Voyage of the Yellow Submarine: A multivoice chronicle of life in a commune,* self-published, 2012.

Dizikes, Peter, "The Meaning of the Butterfly," www.boston.com, June 8, 2008, http://archive.boston.com/bostonglobe/ideas/articles/-2008/06/08/the_meaning_of_the_butterfly/.

Durbin, Kathie, *Bridging a Great Divide: The Battle for the Columbia River Gorge,* Oregon State University Press, Corvallis, Oregon, 2013.

Federal Register, Vol. 45, No. 60, Department of the Interior, Fish and Wildlife Service, "Endangered and Threatened Wildlife and Plants; Reproposal of Critical Habitat for One Species of Butterfly," March 26, 1980.

Federal Register, Vol 45, No. 129, Department of the Interior, Fish and Wildlife Service, "Listing the Oregon Silverspot Butterfly as a Threatened Species With Critical Habitat," July 2, 1980.

Freyfogle, Eric T., "Private Property Rights in Land: An Agrarian View," pp 237-258, in *The Essential Agrarian Reader: The Future of Culture, Community, and the Land,* Norman Wirzha, ed., University Press of Kentucky, 2003.

Freyfogle, Eric T., *On Private Property: Finding Common Ground on the Ownership of Land,* Beacon Press Books, Boston, 2007.

Furnish, Jim, *Toward A Natural Forest The Forest Service in Transition: A Memoir,* OSU Press, Corvallis, 2015.

Hadlow, Robert W., *Elegant Arches, Soaring Spans: C.B. McCullough, Oregon's Master Bridge Builder,* Oregon State University Press, Corvallis, Oregon 2001.

Hammond, Paul C and David McCorkle, "The Decline and Extinction of Speyeria Populations Resulting From Human Environmental Disturbances," *Journal of Research on the Lepidoptera,* pp 217-224, 1983.

Hays, Marjorie H., *The Land That Kept Its Promise (A History of South*

Lincoln County), Lincoln County Historical Society, 1976.

Heilman, Robert Leo, "With A Human Face: When Hoedads Walked the Earth," *History: Oregon Quarterly,* Fall 2011, Eugene, OR.

Hodges, Glenn, "First Americans," *National Geographic,* January 2015, pp.127-137.

Izakson, Orna, "People gather to learn civil disobedience tactics," Newport *News-Times,* August 9, 1995, p. A8.

Izakson, Orna, "Yachats artist arrested in Southern Oregon logging protest," Newport *News-Times,* November 3, 1995, p. A1.

Jeffress, Lynn, Portland Audobon [sic] awards to Ten Mile Association, April 9, 1991 (source unknown).

Johnson, Joseph E., "A Geographic Perspective of the Development of Waldport," Waldport High School, undated.

Keady, Karen, "Tenmile's Voices," *Oregon Coast Magazine,* September/October 1993, pp. 73-76.

Kittell, Joanne and Suzanne Curtis, *The Yachats Indians, Origins of the Yachats Name, and the Reservation Years,* Publication rights held by Confederated Tribes of the Coos, Lower Umpqua, and Siuslaw Indians, and the Confederated Tribes of the Siletz Indians of Oregon, 1996.

Knapp, Gerrit and Arthur C. Nelson, *The Regulated Landscape: Lessons on State Land Use Planning from Oregon,* Lincoln Institute of Land Policy, Cambridge, Massachusetts, 1992.

Laatz, Joan and John Griffith, "Buried Threat," *The Oregonian,* March 30, 1995, p. A15.

Liberty, Robert, "The Battle to Keep Oregon Lovable and Livable: The Story of Tom McCall, Senate Bill 100 and How Oregon Planned Its Growth, 1000 Friends of Oregon," 1998. (tape diskette).

Johnson, Charles K., *Standing at the Water's Edge: Bob Straub's Battle for the Soul of Oregon,* Oregon State University Press, 2012.

Mapes, Jeff, "Andy Kerr, the lightning rod of the Oregon timber wars, now plays behind the scenes role," *The Oregonian/OregonLive,* August 21, 2015.

Marsh, Tom, *To the Promised Land: A History of Government and Politics in Oregon,* Oregon State University Press, Corvallis, Oregon, 2012.

McArthur, Lewis A., *Oregon Geographic Names,* Oregon Historical Society Press, p. 943.

McCorkle, David V., Western Oregon State College, letter to Lane County Board of Commissioners, July 16, 1981.

Nichols, Jackie, "Defending the Coastal Rainforest Nonviolence Training at Ten Mile Creek," *The Oregon Peaceworker,* September 1995, p. 15.

Opler, Paul and Michael Clady, Paul Hammond, Catherine Macdonald, Dennis Murphy, *The Oregon Silverspot Butterfly Revised Recovery Plan.*

Oregon Ballot Measures 37 (2004) and 49 (2007), Wikipedia.

Oregon Department of Forestry Western Lane District, *Factors Affecting Land Use Planning Decisions on Forest Land re: V. Renaghan Request for Plan Amendment and Rezoning,* 1981.

Oregon Zoo Metro, Oregon Silverspot Captive Rearing Procedures, February 1, 2009.

Orr, Elizabeth L. and William N. Orr, *Oregon Geology* 6th Edition, Oregon State University Press, 2012.

Orr, Elizabeth L., William N. Orr, Ewart M. Baldwin, *Geology of Oregon,* 4th ed., Kendall/Hunt Publishing Co. 1992.

Ostrow, Cecelia, *Touching the Earth, Talking to Trees,* self-published, 1990.

Paulson, Janet, "Big Creek Resort project gearing up," *The Siuslaw News,* Vol. 27, No. 31, August 5, 1987.

Pope, Daniel, "A Northwest distaste for nuclear power," *The Seattle Times,* July 31, 2008.

Pope, "Environmental Constraints and Organizational Failures: The Washington Public Power Supply System," Humanities and Social Sciences Online website access December 31, 2011 (http://www.h-net.org/~business/bhcweb/publications/BEHprint/v019/p0074-p0082.pdf).

Provus, Stan, "The Basics of Industrial Development Bonds," *CDFA Spotlight,* Council of Development Finance Agencies.

Radtke, Hans, *Upper Tenmile Creek (Lane County) Homesteaders and Early Settlers,* self-published, November 2015.

Robertson, Lance, "Activists hold off loggers for 4 hours at timber sale," *The Register-Guard,* undated, p. 1B.

Renaghan, Victor J., Letter to Anne Walker, U.S. Fish & Wildlife Service, re Voluntary Actions Taken by Private Landowner at Big Creek, January 30, 2005.

Scale, Zelah, "Tom Smith," *The Minneapolis Star,* August 2, 1975.

Siuslaw National Forest Staff, *Cummins/Tenmile Watershed Analysis,* 1995.

Soper, Curt, Oregon Natural Heritage Program, letter to Michael Copely, January 19, 1981.

Rosetta Stones, "Thunderbird and the Orphan Tsunami: Cascadia 1700." https://blogs.scientificamerican.com/at-scientific-american/HistoryLink.org.

Teutsch, W.L., "Old-Timers Like Old Times," *The Oregon Farmer,* p 3, December 2, 1943.

Tonsfeldt, Ward, *Celebrating the Siuslaw: A Century of Growth,* Discover Your Northwest, 2008.

United States Fish & Wildlife Service, letter to Steve Hopkins, Lane County Land Management Division re Proposal to construct two homes on Victor Renaghan's property within Oregon Silverspot Butterfly habitat at Big Creek, February 13, 2006.

Van Strum, Carol, *A Bitter Fog,* Sierra Club Books, San Francisco, 1983

Vincent, Robert E., letter to Linda and Vic Renaghan, December 13, 1984.

Walker, Mavens & Erickson, Landscape Architects, "Visual Resource Analysis of the Oregon Coastal Zone," Eugene, OR, October 1974.

Walth, Brent, *Fire at Eden's Gate: Tom McCall & The Oregon Story,* Oregon Historical Society Press, 1994.

Welch, Bob, "'Nearly nuclear' anecdotes," *The Register-Guard,* September 4, 2013.

Welch, Craig, "A Brief History of the Spotted-Owl Controversy."

Whereat, Don, *Our Culture and History: The Confederated Tribes of the Coos, Lower Umpqua, and Siuslaw Indians,* Don Whereat, Publisher, 2011.

Whitney, Stephen, *Western Forests,* Alfred A. Knopf, Inc., 1985.

Wilber, Sanford R., Division Chief, Endangered Species, U.S. Fish & Wildlife Service, "Oregon Silverspot Butterfly Conservation Agreement, " August 1, 1983.

Williams, Hill, *The Restless Northwest: A Geological Story;* Washington State University Press, 2002.

Wilson, Edward O., *Anthill: A Novel,* W.W. Norton, 2010.

Yeager, Michael, letter to David McCorkle, December 31, 1980.

ENDNOTES

Introduction

1 The name of the creek, the road, and the community may be spelled Tenmile or Ten Mile. Ten Mile is the official name of the Highway 101 bridge across the creek. Locals always refer to the road, the creek, and the community as Tenmile, one word, with the emphasis on the first syllable. Oregon Geographic Names spells Tenmile as one word and reports that the mouth of the creek is ten miles from its origin on the ridge to the east, but there are several other explanations.

2 Eric T. Freyfogle, *On Private Property: Finding Common Ground on the Ownership of Land*, pp. xix-xiv.

Chapter One

3 Callie McConnell et al, *Cummins/Tenmile Watershed Analysis*, Siuslaw National Forest, 1995, p.1.

4 Jack Sleeper, Fisheries/Aquatic Biologist, Siuslaw National Forest, personal interview, March 13, 2014.

5 Natural Resources Conservation Service, Soil Map—Lane County Area, Oregon (Lower Big Creek),courtesy Karen Bennett, Hydrologist, U.S. Forest Service.

6 Phyllis Steeves, Archaeologist (ret.), Siuslaw National Forest, personal interview, January 8, 2014.

Chapter Two

7 Billie Jo Smith, personal interview, May 13, 2018.

Chapter Three

8 Ellen Morris Bishop, *In Search of Ancient Oregon,* Timber Press, 2003, p. 13.

9 Jim Jackson, Adjunct Professor of Geology (ret), Portland State University, personal interview, June 26, 2014.

10 Jackson, interview.

11 Bishop, *In Search of Ancient Oregon.*

12 Patrick Hughes, *Alfred Wegener,* NASA Earth Observatory website, https://earthobservatory.nasa.gov/Features/Wegener/, February 8, 2001.

13 "Thunderbird and the Orphan Tsunami: Cascadia 1700," https://blogs.scientificamerican.com/at-scientific-american/.

14 Brian Atwood, et al, *The Orphan Tsunami of 1700: Japanese Clues to a Parent Earthquake in North America,* University of Washington Press, January 1, 2005, p. 17.

15 Atwood et al, "Rethinking turbidite paleoseismology along the Cascadia subduction zone," *Geology* (published online), July 29, 2014.

16 Atwood, *The Orphan Tsunami.*

Chapter Four

17 Lance Robertson, Public Affairs, Eugene Water and Electric Board (EWEB), telephone interview, June 13, 2014.

18 Daniel Pope, "A Northwest distaste for nuclear power," *The Seattle Times,* July 31, 2008.

19 Robertson, interview.

20 Site Plan Idealized Cooling Lake for Thermal Power, courtesy Lance Robertson.

21 Artist Conception of #17DACA, courtesy Lance Robertson.

Chapter Five

22 Billie Jo Smith, personal interview, April 14, 2016.

23 Ed and Charlotte Chaney, personal interview, October 1, 2014.

24 Billie Jo Smith, personal interview, April 14, 2016.

25 Lynne Jeffress, "Portland Audobon [sic] awards to Ten Mile Association," newspaper article, publication unknown, April 9, 1991.

[26] Nichols, Jackie, "Defending the Coastal Rainforest Nonviolence Training at Ten Mile Creek," *The Oregon Peaceworker,* September 1995, p. 15.

[27] Billie Jo Smith, personal interview, April 14, 2016.

[28] Marie Cole, personal interview, November 25, 2014.

[29] Chuck Willer, telephone interview, January 5, 2016.

[30] Marie Cole, personal interview, November 25, 2014.

[31] Leon Sterner, personal interview, April 31, 2014.

[32] Sterner, personal interview, April 31, 2014.

[33] Jim Adler, personal interview, April 23, 2016. (Sauna stories are a big part of Tenmile lore. These stories were confirmed by several of the people who were interviewed for this book.)

[34] Ursula Adler, personal interview, April 23, 2016.

[35] Tony Cole, personal interview, April 29, 2014.

Chapter Six

[36] Mary Lou Brown, "Pro—Con: Should a Multi-Million Dollar Resort Be Built in This Undeveloped Coastal Area?" *Oregon Coast Magazine,* June/July 1982.

[37] Lane County Warranty Deed, December 14, 1980.

[38] Public Land Survey System, https://en.wikipedia.org/wiki/Public_Land_Survey_System.

[39] Champ Clark Vaughan, "Willamette Stone and Willamette Meridian," *The Oregon Encyclopedia,* https://oregonencyclopedia.org/articles/willamette_stone_and_willamette_meridian/.

Chapter Seven

[40] *Federal Register,* July 2, 1980, comment of Dr. Lee Miller in Listing the Oregon Silverspot Butterfly as a Threatened Species With Critical Habitat, pp. 44936.

[41] Anne Walker, personal interview, February 17, 2014.

[42] Walker.

[43] Walker.

[44] *Federal Register,* March 26, 1980, Reproposal of Critical Habitat for the Oregon Silverspot Butterfly, p.1984.

[45] *Federal Register,* July 2, 1980, p. 44936-44937.

[46] *Federal Register,* July 2, 1980, p. 44936-44937.

[47] *Federal Register,* July 2, 1980, p. 44936-44937.

[48] *Federal Register,* July 2, 1980, p. 44936-44937.

[49] Walker.

Chapter Eight

[50] Victor Renaghan, quoted in Mary Lou Brown, "Pro and Con," *Oregon Coast Magazine,* June/July 1982, p. 24.

[51] "Pro and Con."

[52] For a complete list of the nineteen goals, see Appendix A.

[53] Victor Renaghan, quoted in "Pro and Con."

[54] Chris Crook, Coastal Planner, Lane County Planning Dept, letter to Michael Yeager, February 11, 1981.

[55] Crook.

[56] Crook.

[57] McCorkle testimony.

[58] Robert Pyle, Letter to WLPC.

[59] Chris Crook, letter to Michael G. Yeager, February 11, 1981.

[60] Joseph R. Blum, Area Manager, U.S. Fish & Wildlife Services, letter to Michael Copely, January 22, 1981.

[61] Michael Yeager, Planning Consultant, WLPC minutes, April 8, 1981.

[62] Jerry MacLeod, Siuslaw District Fish Biologist, letter to Chris Cook, January 23, 1981.

[63] MacLeod.

[64] MacLeod.

[65] Victor Renaghan, WLPC minutes, February 11, 1981.

[66] Larry Bacon, "Dream-come-true development a long way off," Eugene *Register-Guard,* February 13, 1981.

[67] Michael Farthing and Mike Yeager, WLPC minutes, April 11, 1981.

[68] Oregon Department of Forestry Western Lane District, "Factors Affecting Land Use Planning Decisions on Forest Land re: V. Renaghan Request for Plan Amendment and Rezoning," 1981.

[69] Frank Lane, "Douglas fir," *The Oregon Encyclopedia,*" Oregon Historical Society, https://oregonencyclopedia.org/articles/douglas_fir/#.WspDIH8h3Z4.

[70] Ward Tonsfeldt, *Celebrating the Siuslaw: A Century of Growth,* Discover

Your Northwest, 2008.

[71] "Factors Affecting Land Use Planning Decisions on Forest Land re: V. Renaghan Request for Plan Amendment and Rezoning," Oregon State University, Oregon Department of Forestry, Western Lane District, 1981.

[72] OSU, "Factors Affecting Land Use..."

[73] Victor Renaghan, quoted in "Pro and Con," *Oregon Coast Magazine,* June/July 1982, p. 24.

[74] West Lane County Planning Commission, Minutes, February 11, 1981.

[75] WLPC Minutes, February 11, 1981.

[76] WLPC Minutes March 11, 1981.

[77] WLPC Minutes, April 8, 1981.

[78] WLPC Minutes, April 8, 1981.

[79] WLPC Minutes, April 8, 1981.

[80] WLPC Minutes, April 8, 1981.

[81] WLPC Minutes, April 8, 1981.

[82] Bob Warren, personal interview, February 10, 2014.

[83] Warren, interview.

[84] WLPC Minutes, April 8, 1981.

[85] State Land Use Goal 2, (Appendix A).

[86] Lane County Comprehensive Plan.

[87] "Deepening recession the big news of 1981," *Siuslaw News,* December 31, 1981.

[88] WLPC Minutes, April 11, 1981.

[89] WLPC Minutes, April 11, 1981

[90] WLPC Minutes, April 11, 1981.

[91] WLPC Minutes, April 11, 1981.

Chapter Nine

[92] Glenn Hughes, "First Americans," *National Geographic,* January 2015, p. 132.

[93] Hughes, p. 133.

[94] Phyllis Steeves, Archaeologist (ret), Siuslaw National Forest, personal interview, January 8, 2014.

[95] Steeves.

[96] Steeves.

[97] Jesse Beers, Cultural Director, Confederated Tribes of Coos, Lower Umpqua, and Siuslaw Indians, telephone interview.

[98] Don Whereat, *Our Culture and History: The Confederated Tribes of the Coos, Lower Umpqua, and Siuslaw Indians.* Most of this account of Native American history on the Central Oregon Coast is from this excellent resource book.

[99] Joanne Kittel and Suzanne Curtis, *The Yachats Indians, Origins of the Yachats Name, and the Reservation Years,* 1996.

Chapter Ten

[100] Stephen D. Puter, *Looters of the Public Domain,* quoted in Ward Tonsfeldt, *Celebrating the Siuslaw: A Century of Growth,* Discover Your Northwest, 2008, p. 22.

[101] Tonsfeldt, *Celebrating the Siuslaw: A Century of Growth,* pp. 26-38.

[102] The Siuslaw National Forest Digital Archive, https://oregondigital.org/sets/siuslaw#.

[103] Marjorie Hays, *The Land That Kept Its Promise (A History of South Lincoln County),* Lincoln County Historical Society, 1976.

[104] Tonsfeldt, p. 24.

[105] Hans Radtke, *Upper Tenmile Creek (Lane County) Homesteaders and Early Settlers,* self-published, November 2015, p. 21.

[106] Stan Poe, video interview by Hans Radtke, Upper Tenmile Creek (Lane County), *Homesteaders and Early Settlers,* November 2015.

[107] Barbara Beck Bogue, *Proved Up On Ten Mile Creek,* 1986, pp. 48-49.

[108] Bogue, p. 19.

[109] Bogue, p. 23.

[110] Bogue, p. 15.

[111] Hays, p. 52.

[112] Thompson, p. 44.

[113] Thompson, p. 44.

[114] Thompson, p.56-57.

[115] Bogue, pp. 65-72.

[116] Bogue, pp. 48-58.

[117] Susanna Beck Yunker, personal interview.

[118] Lane County Land Management Division, Big Creek archive. All available warranty deeds were reviewed, but the record is

incomplete. Requests for copies by Victor Renaghan's lawyer indicate that some of the microfiche reels were illegible. Specifically, I was unable to trace how the property came down to Hugh and Marguerite Sherwood, who sold the Big Creek property to Victor and Linda Renaghan.

[119] Warranty Deed, Reel 420, No. 49455, cited in letter to Mike Farthing, December 14, 1990.

[120] Warranty Deed, Reel 1110, No. 63574, cited in letter to Mike Farthing, December 14, 1990.

Chapter Eleven

[121] Brent Walth, *Fire at Eden's Gate,* p. 314.

[122] Walth, p. 181.

[123] Tom Marsh, *To the Promised Land,* p. 283.

[124] Walth, p. 356.

[125] Sy Adler, *Oregon Plans,* pp 40-41. Sy Adler, professor of urban studies at Portland State University, provides a detailed history of the development of SB100 and how it changed land use planning in Oregon forever.

126 S. Adler, p. 50.

127 Matt Spangler, Senior Coastal Policy Analyst, Oregon Coastal Management Program, LCDC, personal interview, July 1, 2014.

128 S. Adler p. 86-87.

129 S. Adler, p. 35.

130 S. Adler, p. 35.

131 S. Adler, p. 35.

132 S. Adler, p. 39.

133 Walth, pp. 357-358.

[134] Spangler, personal interview.

[135] S. Adler, pp 45-50.

[136] S. Adler, p 127.

[137] Steve Schell, quoted in *Oregon Plans,* p.128-129.

[138] *Oregon Coastal Management Program,* pp. 1-3.

[139] Dorothy Anderson, League of Women Voters, quoted in *Oregon Plans,* p 72.

[140] S. Adler, p. 73.

[141] Goal 1, Citizen Involvement (see Appendix A).

[142] Kent Howe, Planning Director (ret.), Lane County, personal interview, March 5, 2015.

[143] Howe.

[144] Howe.

Chapter Twelve

[145] Cecelia Ostrow, "The Story of Walt," *Touching the Earth Talking to Trees: Mystical Experiences in the Old Growth Forest,* 1990, Cecelia Ostrow, pp 27-58. The account of Ed and Cecelia's involvement in the Big Creek campaign is found in *Touching the Earth,* in which Cecelia refers to Ed as "Walt," who started his own organization, the Natural Earth Foundation, and worked with Friends of the Oregon Coast (FOC) to stop the resort development. The conflicts that arose between "Walt" and FOC were corroborated in personal interviews with Billie Jo Smith and others involved with FOC, many of whom are mentioned in Cecelia's account. She also slips once (p. 55) using the name Ed rather than Walt. In April 1991, Cecelia inscribed a copy of her book and gave it to Tom Smith. I have used "Walt's" real name and modified some of the dialogue to correspond to more normal usage.

[146] Ostrow, p. 49.

[147] *Register-Guard,* Affidavit of publication, July 6, 1981.

[148] Certification of Mailing, July 15, 1981.

[149] Ostrow, p. 51.

[150] Ostrow, p. 37.

[151] Ostrow, p. 53.

[152] Ostrow, pp. 63-64.

[153] Andy Kerr, personal interview, October 29, 2014.

[154] James Montieth, telephone interview, March 21, 2016.

[155] Jeff Mapes, "Andy Kerr, the lightning rod of the Oregon timber wars, now plays behind the scenes role," *The Oregonian/OregonLive,* August 21, 2015.

[156] Mapes.

[157] Kerr.

[158] Montieth.

[159] Montieth.

[160] Kerr.

[161] Ostrow, p. 50.

[162] Ostrow, p. 52-53.

[163] Alexis Petrohilos, letters to the editor, Eugene *Register-Guard* (date unknown).

[164] Petrohilos.

[165] Tom Smith, Letter to Harold Rutherford, Chair, Board of County Commissioners, September 25, 1981.

[166] Gerald Rust, Letter to the Editor, *Siuslaw News*, publication date unknown.

[167] Editorial, *The Siuslaw News*, September 13, 1981.

[168] Harold Rutherford, Chair, Board of County Commissioners, Letters to the Editor, *The Siuslaw News*, September 24, 1981.

[169] Larry Bacon, "Opponents move to block coastal resort complex," Eugene *Register-Guard*, September 4, 1981. RG 9/4/81.

[170] Findings of Fact and Conclusions, WZC 81-03.

[171] Findings of Fact.

[172] Findings of Fact.

[173] David McCorkle, Western Oregon State College, Letter to Lane County Board of Commissioners, July 16, 1981.

[174] Robert M. Pyle, Lepidoptera Specialist Group, Letter to WLPC, February 23, 1981.

[175] James Monteith, Executive Director, Oregon Wilderness Coalition, Letter to Board of Commissioners, September 28, 1981.

[176] Findings of Fact.

[177] Findings of Fact.

[178] Findings of Fact.

[179] Monteith, telephone interview.

[180] Ostrow, p. 53.

[181] Ostrow, p. 53.

[182] Bob Warren, personal interview.

[183] Warren.

[184] Billie Jo Smith, personal interview.

[185] Van Vactor, memo to Board of County Commissioners.

[186] Van Vactor, memo to Board of County Commissioners.

Chapter Thirteen

[187] Jim Adler, personal interview.

[188] J. Adler.

[189] Tim Sercombe, personal interview, June 19, 2014.

[190] Petition to LUBA re County Commissioners' decision, Nov. 25, 1981.

[191] LUBA request for additional information, November 25, 1981.

[192] Tim Sercombe, letter to Tony and Ginger Cole, May 7, 1982.

[193] Sercombe, interview.

[194] Sercombe, interview.

[195] S. Adler, p. 30.

[196] Sercombe, interview.

[197] Tom McCall.

[198] Sercombe, interview.

[199] LUBA No. 81-102 Warren et al vs Lane County et al, August 12, 1985.

[200] Sercombe, interview.

[201] FOC Meeting Minutes, January 22, 1982.

[202] J. Adler, interview.

[203] Robert Leo Heilman, "With a Human Face: When Hoedads Walked the Earth," rlheilman@frontier.com

[204] Descriptions of FOC fundraising activities came from interviews with several members of FOC.

[205] Warren et al vs. Lane County, No. 81-102, CA A25365, decided April 21, 1983.

[206] Sercombe, interview.

[207] Warren et al vs. Lane County, 686 p.2d 31.6 (1984).

[208] Sercombe, interview.

[209] Sercombe, interview.

Chapter Fourteen

[210] Larry Bacon, "Big Creek seeks state aid; opponents get court review," Eugene *Register-Guard*, February 28, 1984.

[211] Bacon, "Big Creek seeks state aid…"

[212] Bacon, "Big Creek seeks state aid…"

[213] Bacon, "Big Creek seeks state aid…"

[214] Hans Radtke, personal interview, January 31, 2014.

[215] Radtke, interview.

[216] Robert Ackerman, personal interview, January 14, 2014.

[217] Ackerman, interview.

[218] Daniel Jack Chasan:, *The Fall of the House of WPPSS*, Sasquatch Publishing, 1985.

[219] Daniel Pope, "Environmental Constraints and Organizational Failures: The Washington Public Power Supply System," *Humanities and Social Sciences Online* website access December 31, 2011 (http://www.h-net.org/~business/bhcweb/publications/BEHprint/v019/p0074-p0082.pdf.)

[220] Billie Jo Smith, personal interview, April 23, 2016.

[221] Jim Boyd, "County OKs Big Creek request," Eugene *Register-Guard,* April 12, 1984.

[222] Boyd.

[223] Boyd.

[224] Boyd.

[225] Boyd.

[226] Scott Lieuallen, telephone interview, January 8, 2016.

[227] Lieuallen.

[228] Ackerman, interview. (Document not available).

[229] Nathan Buehler, telephone interview, Oregon4Biz staff.

[230] Vic Renaghan, quoted by Larry Bacon, "Developer vows to finish project," Eugene *Register-Guard,* September 12, 1984.

[231] Ackerman.

[232] Ackerman.

[233] Ackerman.

[234] Ackerman.

[235] Ackerman.

[236] Ackerman.

[237] http://www.oregon4biz.com?Business-financing-resources/Oregon-Finance-Programs/Oregon-Industrial-Development-Bonds/.

[238] Ackerman, letter to EDC, re: Big Creek Project, May 23, 1984.

[239] http://www.oregon4biz.com?Business-financing-resources/Oregon-Finance-Programs/Oregon-Industrial-Development-Bonds/.

[240] Ackerman, re: Big Creek Project, May 23, 1984.

[241] Ackerman, re: Big Creek Project, May 23, 1984.

[242] Ackerman, re: Big Creek Project, May 23, 1984.

[243] Ackerman, interview.

[244] In re Primus, https://supreme.justia.com/cases/federal/
     us/436/412/case.html

[245] Andy Kerr, personal interview, October 29, 2014.

[246] http://www.oregon4biz.com?Business-financing-resources/Oregon-
     Finance-Programs/Oregon-Industrial-Development-Bonds/.

Chapter Fifteen

[247] Paul Engelmeyer, personal interview, January 24, 2014.

[248] Bob Warren, personal interview, February 10, 2014.

[249] Bob Warren, memo re Forest Service appraisal, August 13, 1991.

[250] Bob warren, personal interview.

[251] Robert W. Hadlow, *Elegant Arches, Soaring Spans: C.B .McCullough,
     Oregon's Master Bridge Builder*, Oregon State University Press, 2001,
     p. 42.

[252] Hadlow, p. 80.

[253] Hadlow, p. 82-83.

[254] Hadlow, p. 83.

[255] Bob Warren, personal interview.

[256] Oregon Shores Conservation Coalition,
     https://oregonshores.org/about/history.

[257] Billie Jo Smith, personal interview.

[258] Billie Jo Smith, interview.

[259] Billie Jo Smith, interview.

[260] Billie Jo Smith, interview.

[261] Stacy Smith, personal interview, March 20, 2016.

[262] Stacy Smith.

[263] Alison Clement, "Burial," unpublished essay.

[264] Billie Jo Smith, interview.

[265] Clement.

[266] Alice Walker, *The Temple of My Familiar,* Weidenfeld & Nicolson,
     Harcourt, 1989.

[267] Clement.

[268] Clement.

[269] Paul Engelmeyer, personal interview.

[270] Derek Johnson, personal interview, February 26, 2016.

271 Kent Howe, personal interview.

272 Keith Ellingson, Lane County Land Management Dept, memo re PA0169-90, Partition Big Creek, February 5, 1991.

273 Gary Hostick, District Wildlife Biologist, ODFW, memo to Roy Burns, planning director, February 8, 1991.

274 Michael E. Farthing, Memo to Chris Fromme, Marineau & Associates re: Appraisal of Big Creek Property, April 11, 1990.

275 Michael Copely, Lane County Land Management Division, memo to Lane County Hearings Official, December 2, 1992 re PA0169-91.

276 Copely memo, December 2, 1992.

277 Michael Farthing, memo to Planning Department.

278 Victor Renaghan, quoted in "Pro and Con."

279 Findings of Fact and Conclusions, WZC 81-03.

280 Michael Farthing, letter to Chris Fromme, Marineau & Associates, April 11, 1990.

281 Farthing to Fromme.

282 Spangler, interview.

283 Victor Renaghan, memo to hearings officer, November, 1992.

284 Farthing memo to Lane County Land Management Division.

285. Renaghan, letter to Lane County Hearings Official, November 17, 1992, p. 3.

286 Renaghan, letter to Lane County Hearings Official, November 17, 1992, p. 3.

287 Renaghan, letter to Lane County Hearings Official, p 10.

288 Renaghan, letter to Lane County Hearings Official, p. 4.

289 Renaghan, letter to Lane County, Hearings Official, p 6.

290 Renaghan, letter to Lane County Hearings Official, p. 11.

291 Renaghan, telephone interview.

292 Renaghan, letter to Lane County Hearings Official, p. 12.

293 Renaghan, letter to Lane County Hearings Official, p. 7.

294 Renaghan, letter to Lane County Planning Department.

295 Jim Adler, letter to Lane County Land Management Division, date unknown. (This document was not in the files.)

296 Renaghan, letter to Gary Darnielle, Lane County Hearings Official, p. 1, undated.

297 J. Adler, interview. (Copy of letter unavailable).

[298] Michael Copely, memo to Lane County Hearings Official, December 2, 1992.

[299] Renaghan, letter to Lane County Planning Department.

[300] Renaghan, letter to Lane County Hearings Official, p. 2.

[301] Renaghan, letter to Lane County Hearings Official, p. 1, undated.

[302] Renaghan, letter to Gail McEwan, Lane County Planning Department, undated but sent with cover letter from Michael Farthing dated January 20, 1993.

[303] Renaghan, notice to Hearings Officer withdrawing application, August 2, 1993.

[304] Lane County Public Works Department, Land Management Division, July 5, 1994.

[305] Keir Miller, Lane County Land Management Division, telephone interview, December 10, 2014.

[306] Keir Miller, Lane County Land Management Division, telephone interview, December 10, 2014.

[307] Tom McCall.

[308] See Appendix A.

[309] S. Adler, p. 105.

[310] Voters Pamphlet, vol. 1 state measures, Oregon Department of State, November 2, 2004, pp. 103-132.

[311] Voters Pamphlet, vol. 1, pp. 103-132.

[312] Voters Pamphlet, vol. 1, pp. 103-132.

[313] Voters Pamphlet, vol. 1, pp. 103-132.

[314] Voters Pamphlet, vol. 1, pp. 103-132.

[315] Voters Pamphlet, vol. 1, pp. 103-132.

[316] Voters Pamphlet, vol. 1, pp. 103-132.

[317] Oregon Ballot Measures 37 (2004) and 49 (2007), https://en.wikipedia.org/wiki/Oregon_Ballot_Measures_37_(2004)_and_49_(2007).

[318] Derek Johnson, personal interview, January 18, 2016.

[319] Dale Saari, Windemere Real Estate, Letter to Victor Renaghan, April 22, 2006.

[320] Saari.

[321] Saari.

[322] Saari.

[323] Keir Miller, personal interview.

[324] Miller.

[325] Miller.

[326] Jim Adler, personal interview, February 27, 2014.

[327] J. Adler, interview.

[328] Anne Walker, interview.

[329] An earlier memorandum of agreement signed on July 24, 1989 had deeded the portion of the property west of Highway 101 to The Nature Conservancy. Reel 1588, Nol. 36062, Lane County Land Management Division.

[330] Johnson.

[331] Johnson. (Note: some of the material was included in the county file, of which I copied more than 800 pages.)

[332] Johnson.

[333] Johnson.

[334] Johnson.

[335] Johnson.

[336] Johnson.

[337] I'm indebted to Derek Johnson at The Nature Conservancy for the detailed history of the Big Creek transaction.

[338] Engelmeyer, interview.

[339] *Big Creek site visit with Peter DeFazio,* Milo Graamans videographer, August 20, 2013. https://audubonportland.org/news/sept23-2013.

[340] *Big Creek site visit with Peter DeFazio.*

[341] *Big Creek site visit with Peter DeFazio.*

[342] *Big Creek site visit with Peter DeFazio.*

[343] Peter Dizikes, "The Meaning of the Butterfly," *www.Boston.com, June 8, 2008.* http://archive.boston.com/bostonglobe/ideas/articles/2008/06/08/the_meaning_of_the_butterfly/

[344] Ray Bradbury, "A Sound of Thunder," *Golden Apples of the Sun,* 1953. See also https://genius.com/Ray-bradbury-a-sound-of-thunder-annotated.

ABOUT THE AUTHOR

ANDREA SCHARF has been writing since she was ten. She has an MFA in creative writing from Vermont College of Fine Arts, and has published short stories and articles on subjects ranging from the nutritional impact of dead salmon to the financial impact of a colliers' strike.

Her reading interests include fiction and nonfiction. She also writes a blog about what she reads, which can be found at https://andreasbookblog.wordpress.com/.

She has worked as a teacher, co-founder and manager of Portland's Saturday Market, as a small business entrepreneur, city planner, marketing director, and association manager, among other positions. Whether hiking in the Cascades or the Coast Range, exploring tide pools, or walking through an urban park, she is always attracted to the natural world. Since moving to the Oregon Coast, she has been active in protecting that world as founder and chair of View the Future, a nonprofit environmental advocacy organization.

Andrea lives on the Yachats River, just beyond the fog zone.